T0357861

"This book is a fresh and unique study on G[...]
had thought of it myself! *The Law, the Chri[...]
both personal and group study. R. L. Solber[...]
Galatians, apply it to their lives, and defend it [...]

—**SEAN MCDOWELL**, PhD, associate professor of apologetics,
Biola University, author of more than 20 books, popular YouTuber

"Solberg reintroduces the book of Galatians through an apologetic lens that offers fresh insight and practical application to equip today's readers. He affirms that the book of Galatians still speaks to today's politically charged space in which the church is in danger of shrinking back due to prevailing false gospels. We hear Paul's voice as Solberg unpacks the verses and provides an understanding of Paul's heart behind his words: that God's people would not be led astray by false teachers, which could also be themselves."

—**DENISE PASS**, PhD in biblical exposition, speaker, author of *Make Up Your Mind: Unlock Your Thoughts, Transform Your Life* and *Shame Off You*

"Prof. Solberg writes passionately yet humbly on Galatians, a perennial New Testament book of vast theological and existential importance. His study is highly recommended to all who take the Christian Scriptures and the Gospel of Christ seriously."

—**DR. GIORGOS KALANTZIS**, professor of philosophy and apologetics, Greek Bible College, Athens, Greece

"In *The Law, the Christ, the Promise*, R. L. Solberg offers a profound, verse-by-verse journey through Galatians that equips readers to seek and resiliently defend a Christ-centered faith with clarity and conviction. His deep respect for Scripture shines through as he helps believers discern the true gospel amid modern cultural currents. This book is a powerful tool for anyone eager to understand why we believe the gospel and how to respond to false teachings with gentleness and wisdom."

—**DARREN WHITEHEAD**, senior pastor, Church of the City, Nashville, Tennessee, author of *The Digital Fast: Detox Your Mind and Reclaim What Matters Most*

"There is no shortage of works on the apostle Paul's magnificent letter to the Galatians. This engaging study stands out due to its probing questions about the nature of the Christian faith. Solberg capably guides readers through the text of Galatians, offering keen insight regarding Paul's understanding of the gospel message, the development and character of his arguments, and the contemporary relevance of his instruction. This study allows Paul to speak for himself about his core convictions and the manner in which believers are to live as the new creation. Solberg is to be commended for producing a valuable resource that is sure to encourage and strengthen the faith of many."

—BENJAMIN LAIRD, professor of biblical studies,
John W. Rawlings School of Divinity, Liberty University

"Solberg's *The Law, the Christ, and the Promise* takes us into the context of Paul's spirited letter to the believers in Galatia. Solberg masterfully compares and contrasts the text of Galatians to the rest of the Scriptures to help us see a deeper and richer meaning behind this epistle. This book is a great addition to the shelves of any believer, from theologians and pastors to missionaries and anyone who has a passion to strengthen their understanding of the Word."

—DR. DAN SERED, chief operating officer, Jews for Jesus, president,
the Lausanne Consultation on Jewish Evangelism (LCJE)

"With approachable style and theologically balanced views, this examination of the book of Galatians is thorough, trustworthy, and insightful. This book will challenge the reader to investigate the Scriptures and apply each aspect of Paul's epistle to their lives."

—DANNY WILLIAMSON, director, Speaking Louder
Ministries, author of *Where's the Joy?*

"R. L. Solberg has blended apologetic and exegetical concerns into a timely commentary on Galatians. He has provided a relevant, clear, and engaging source answering questions of the faith through the text of Galatians."

—RICHARD ALAN FUHR JR., professor of
biblical studies, Liberty University

"Paul offers a punchy and edgy apologetic toward the Judaizing heretics in the book of Galatians. In similar fashion Solberg offers a punchy and edgy commentary that reads more like a passionate and theologically robust sermon than a boring lecture. I only regret that this book was not already written when I preached through Galatians myself."

—JOSHUA LEWIS, pastor, King's Fellowship Church, host, Remnant Radio

"To quote the author, 'Apologetics is not about winning arguments, scoring points, or proving the other guy wrong; it's about saving souls.' Solberg's conviction of 'defending truth' and 'pointing people to the gospel of Jesus' is evident throughout this fascinating journey in Paul's letter to the Galatians. Solberg has a unique gift of transforming a first-century letter of instruction to a small group of early Christian converts into a life map for our own present voyage. He so clearly highlights this still-relevant truth: 'a person is not justified by the works of the law, but by faith in Jesus Christ' (Gal. 2:16)."

—REV. MARK BUSHUIAKOVISH, pastor, Our Savior Lutheran Church, Nashville, Tennessee

"As a pastor, I'm always on the lookout for resources that are biblically faithful and engage the head, the heart, and the hands. R. L. Solberg's unique apologetics approach to the book of Galatians does just that and reflects his personality: bold, compelling, and clear. Every pastor and serious student of the New Testament needs this work."

-DR. JAY STROTHER, senior pastor, Brentwood Baptist Church, Tennessee

"The most powerful theological apologetics are those deeply rooted in and drawing directly from Scripture. R. L. Solberg masterfully exemplifies this approach in *The Law, the Christ, the Promise*. He meticulously guides readers through Paul's arguments in Galatians, thoughtfully exegeting analogies, unpacking powerful imagery, and addressing challenging theological issues. I strongly recommend this book to anyone seeking either a biblically grounded apologetic against a works-righteousness movement or a deeper, more insightful understanding of Scripture."

—ERIC HERNANDEZ, apologetics lead and millennial specialist, The Baptist General Convention of Texas

"R. L. Solberg's *The Law, the Christ, the Promise* offers a clear and compelling exploration of the intersection between law and grace in Christian theology. Through his thoughtful apologetic approach to the book of Galatians, Solberg skillfully dismantles legalism while providing a balanced critique of antinomianism. His scholarly yet accessible treatment invites readers to a deeper understanding of how faith in Christ harmonizes with biblical law. I can't wait to share this book with my LifeGroup!"

—EDWARD M. SMITH, president, Williamson College

"I've served the local church for more than forty years in multiple positions, from senior pastor to director of men's ministry, and I found Solberg's theological insights on the book of Galatians both encouraging and educational. His writings and voice are needed in the modern church, and you will find comfort and wisdom in his words."

—PASTOR PAUL GUFFEY

The Law,
the Christ,
the Promise

The Law,
The Christ,
The Promise

A VERSE-BY-VERSE
APOLOGETICS
BIBLE STUDY THROUGH
GALATIANS

R. L. Solberg

ZONDERVAN
REFLECTIVE

ZONDERVAN REFLECTIVE

The Law, the Christ, the Promise
Copyright © 2025 by R. L. Solberg

Published in Grand Rapids, Michigan, by Zondervan. Zondervan is a registered trademark of The Zondervan Corporation, L.L.C., a wholly owned subsidiary of HarperCollins Christian Publishing, Inc.

Requests for information should be addressed to customercare@harpercollins.com.

Zondervan titles may be purchased in bulk for educational, business, fundraising, or sales promotional use. For information, please email SpecialMarkets@Zondervan.com.

ISBN 978-0-31016586-6 (audio)

Library of Congress Cataloging-in-Publication Data

Names: Solberg, R. L. (Robert L.), 1969- author.
Title: The law, the Christ, the promise: a verse-by-verse apologetics Bible study through Galatians / R.L. Solberg.
Description: Grand Rapids, Michigan: Zondervan Reflective, [2025]
Identifiers: LCCN 2024039573 (print) | LCCN 2024039574 (ebook) | ISBN 9780310165842 (paperback) | ISBN 9780310165859 (ebook)
Subjects: LCSH: Bible. Galatians--Commentaries. | Paul, the Apostle, Saint. | Apologetics. | BISAC: RELIGION / Christian Theology / Apologetics | RELIGION / Christian Ministry / Discipleship
Classification: LCC BS2685.53 .S65 2025 (print) | LCC BS2685.53 (ebook) | DDC 227/.407--dc23/eng/20240925
LC record available at https://lccn.loc.gov/2024039573
LC ebook record available at https://lccn.loc.gov/2024039574

Interior design: Sara Colley

Printed in the United States of America

24 25 26 27 28 LBC 5 4 3 2 1

To Debra, the Brave, my ezer kenegdo.

CONTENTS

Part I: Paul, the Church Historian

Part II: Paul, the Theology Professor

Part III: Paul, the Concerned Pastor

FOREWORD

The most memorable lectures of my seminary education were the unplanned kind—what you might call "unlectures." Most classes were systematic lessons on dogmatics, exegesis, or church history. These were helpful but could be a bit ho-hum at times. We still needed them—and got them. But once in a blue moon, a spark would land inside the heart of the professor, and—boy, oh boy—look out! He flamed with rhetorical zeal. The teacher would pace back and forth at the front of the classroom, firing off passionate speech. Five, ten, fifteen minutes would fly by. We just sat there, mesmerized. No one dared scribble any notes lest we miss something. This was too important—so we just drank it all in. To this day, thirty years later, I can close my eyes and still hear those robust unlectures.

Almost without exception, these passionate words were about the things that matter most.

Galatians is the unlecture of Professor Paul. Open up your Bible to that epistle and touch the page. So many centuries later, these words, inked with apostolic fire, are still warm to the touch. Many say that the most comprehensive treatment of Christian theology in the New Testament is Romans. I have no dispute with that. But Galatians, with its vivacity and edge, is arguably Paul's finest epistle. Why? He weds heady theology to the hearty zeal of an apostolic pastor. He is writing about the things that matter most—that matter to him, that *should* matter to the Galatians, and, most importantly, that matter to God.

And these things still matter to us. If we strip aside the unique peculiarities of the goings-on in the Galatian congregations, we see that what was happening to them is the perennial temptation wooing the hearts of all believers: to assume that our right standing with God is based on "shoulds" and "musts" and "attaboys." People think, "If only I do _____ or refrain from doing _____, Jesus will give me the heavenly high-five." Or perhaps they reason, "Between the work of Jesus plus my acts of obedience, salvation is a sure thing." If we fill in those blanks or buy into the lie of "Jesus + Me," we welcome the gospel-destroying music of the Judaizing band.

In Galatians, Paul obliterates these syncretistic lyrics that insist God must enlist the help of sinners to save sinners. Do we need to circumcise males or obey any of the unique dictates of the old covenant to get right or stay right with God? "No," Paul says. We are not under Sinai but atop Calvary. Shall we observe the new covenant's law of love as Christians? "Yes, of course," the apostle affirms. But, even then, does our loving of our neighbor sustain or in any way contribute to our salvation? No, of course not! We are saved by Christ alone. We are kept in salvation by Christ alone. In Galatians, Paul insists that the only skin in the game of salvation is on the body of Jesus—and it bears the crucifixion scars of love.

The freedom message of Galatians is evergreen. Each generation of the church revels in this message. Each generation must also take in hand the liberating key of this epistle and go boldly to those places where teachers, denominations, or movements have revived the old Judaizing locks and chains. The ideal candidates for teaching Galatians are those not only deeply rooted in the Scriptures and zealous for the gospel but also gifted rhetorically and driven by a genuine love and concern for people. They will be debaters who are unafraid to contend for the truth yet seek to liberate the captives, not score points. They will be the kind of people who, in head and heart, know and care about the things that matter most.

Robert Solberg is such a person. He is a Galatians man. And this book, this exemplary book, is his gift to readers. I know Rob. I have sat at the table with him, watched his videos, and read his books. I recommend his materials to people frequently and unhesitatingly. Recently, while I was on a speaking trip a couple approached me, joyful tears streaming from both their faces, to tell me what an impact Rob's ministry had made on their lives. They are but two of the thousands who would echo the same happy and grateful words.

So, open up the book of Galatians. Keep turning the pages of *The Law, the Christ, the Promise*. Listen to the passionate unlecture of Paul. Ponder the insights, apologetic arguments, and keen insights of Robert Solberg. As you do, say a prayer of thanks along with me for the freedom we have in Jesus and for all those who, like Rob, faithfully wave the banner of the good news of salvation in Christ and Christ alone.

CHAD BIRD

Scholar in residence for 1517, author of
Hitchhiking with Prophets

WHY GALATIANS MATTERS TODAY

My parents tell me I was something of a precocious child, inquisitive to the point of challenging. While I cannot validate such rumors, I do remember being curious about almost everything. *Why is lying wrong? How do they get the music to come out of the radio? Why do I have to go to bed if I'm not tired?* I vividly remember the frustration of my unstoppable line of questioning colliding with the immovable declaration "Because I said so." That statement so vexed my young soul that I vowed never to curse my own children with such a dreadfully unsatisfying answer.

Of course, as I matured, I came to realize that all the world is not a debate stage and not every moment is suitable for a robust interrogation. However, my questioning persisted, grew, and eventually took a theological turn. *How do we know there is a God and that He loves us? How do we know Jesus existed or what He really said? How does believing the right thing lead to eternal salvation?* These questions ultimately brought me to what I refer to in hindsight as "practical atheism." I never formally denounced belief in God; I just stopped thinking about Him altogether. I figured God could do His thing and I would do mine. (Bear with me. I'm getting to Galatians.)

Not until I got married at the tender age of twenty-two did

I begin to sense there must be something more. My deep love for my wife, Debra, opened my eyes to the possibility that life isn't all about me. I recognized that there was something bigger out there—something more significant and more real than my little world. When our first child arrived a few years later, it was all over for me.

I will never forget staring into the beautiful face of my minutes-old daughter, Sami, the physical embodiment of the miracle of life. God began to make sense to me in a new way. This wasn't head knowledge; I was experiencing love in its purest form, the kind of love you give without expecting anything in return. I was suddenly prepared to die if that was what it took to keep my child safe and secure.

Something happened in my soul. The penny dropped. The realization dawned on me that, like a faint echo of God, I, too, was a father. I, too, participated in the creation of a life. The big blue eyes staring up at me belonged to a tiny human being who did not exist a year ago. I instantly wanted every good thing for her and was willing to go to the ends of the earth to save her if necessary. Not because of anything she had done. Rather, because of who she is and *whose* she is: mine. Where did this kind of love come from? And how was it possible that when this miracle repeated itself three years later with our second daughter, Maggie, my love wasn't divided in half but doubled?

I wish I could tell you that my life was all puppies and rainbows after these revelations and my faith in God soared like the saints of old. The truth is that my questions persisted even after my faith was renewed. *If faith in Jesus is the only path to salvation, what about everyone who believed in God before He was born? Can you believe in Jesus, get your ticket to heaven, and then just live however you want? How can God look at us and not remember all the sinful things we've done?*

What I have come to love about the Christian faith—and the book of Galatians is a shining example—is that it does not require us to check our intellect at the door and adopt a blind faith. Scripture reveals again and again that God welcomes honest questions, challenges, and even debates. In fact, the name God gave His ancient people, Israel, means "wrestles with God."[1] The one Person in the universe who actually has the right to answer "Because I said so" often invites us instead to wrestle with Him. "Come now, let us reason together, says the Lord" (Isa. 1:18 ESV). The Bible says we are to love God not just with our heart, soul, and strength, but also with our minds.[2]

I leaned into that aspect of my walk with God. I read widely and kicked hard on the load-bearing walls of my faith to make sure they were sound. This led me to the theological discipline of apologetics and the unique approach we will take in this study of the book of Galatians. (More on apologetics in a moment.) My favorite questions are still "how?" and "why?" And for such a short epistle, Galatians tackles a number of big questions about the Christian faith:

- Why do Paul's writings have any authority? Was he really an apostle?
- How are we made right with God? How do we become children of God?
- What is the difference between a false gospel and the real gospel?
- What is the relationship between the law and grace? Between faith and works?
- Why was the law given in the first place? Is it still in effect? If so, which laws still apply to us? What about the Ten Commandments?
- What has changed under the new covenant?
- Is there a distinction between Jews and Gentiles in the church?
- What does it mean to live a Spirit-led life?

- What does it mean to have freedom in Christ?
- What happened to Paul after his encounter with Jesus? Who taught him the gospel?
- Does the life of Abraham even matter to twenty-first century Christians?
- How should communities of faith treat one another? How should they handle disagreements? How should they handle false teachers in their midst?

These questions (and more) are expertly addressed by the apostle Paul in his fiery letter to the believers in Galatia. To our great blessing, God did not command us to believe in Jesus "Because I said so!" Instead, like a loving Father, He gave His church His written Word, including the masterpiece we know as Galatians. He must have known that, even in the twenty-first century, some of us would still have questions.

INTRODUCTION[1]

There are many fantastic commentaries on the book of Galatians available today. This is not one of them. By that I mean this is not a commentary in the traditional sense. The book you hold in your hands is a verse-by-verse *apologetic* Bible study. Apologetics is a branch of theology dedicated to defending Christian truth claims against critics and false teachings. Its name comes from the Greek word *apologia*, which means "to make a defense, desire to clear yourself." The apostle Peter wrote:

> In your hearts revere Christ as Lord. Always be prepared to give an answer [*apologia*] to everyone who asks you to give the reason for the hope that you have. But do this with gentleness and respect. (1 Peter 3:15)

The first apologists were the New Testament (NT) authors. Chief among them was the apostle Paul, whose letter to the churches in Galatia offers us a master class in theology, biblical history, pastoral passion, and, yes, apologetics. What makes this Bible study unique is its focused exploration of the text from the apologetics perspective.

In our modern, post-Christian information era, defending the truth of Christianity is more important than ever. And the discipline of apologetics serves three important roles. First, it strengthens the faith of believers by teaching us why we believe what we believe. It points us to the biblical and theological foundations that undergird the doctrines and teachings of Christianity. And Galatians is a wealth of such foundational truths. Apologetics helps the body of Christ remain "in line with the truth of the gospel" (2:14). It serves as a regulating function in the theology of the church, helping us to avoid drifting away on the current of modern culture.

Second, apologetics helps identify ideas about the gospel and our relationship with God that may seem wonderful at first glance but turn out to be wrong and dangerous. Such are the false teachings Paul wrote against in this epistle. Studying his letter through an apologetic lens consequently helps us to become wise and discerning Christians. The more familiar we are with the genuine gospel, the lower the chance we will be duped by a counterfeit.

Third, apologetics helps doubters and unbelievers clear away myths, misunderstandings, and untrue beliefs that can cloud our view of God and the gospel. It allows us to see Jesus more accurately and respond to the real Christ rather than a false distortion. In this way, apologetics helps attract people to the true gospel. This is a vital task in our current scientific age where doubt and misinformation run rampant.

At this point, I need to make a full disclosure to the reader. I am not a Christian apologist because my faith is so strong, but because my intellectual questions are so persistent. I identify with the father of the healed child who cried out to Jesus, "I do believe; help me overcome my unbelief!" (Mark 9:24). I study the Bible and pursue apologetics to continually remind myself and others of the unshakeable truth of the living God.

That is the heart with which we are approaching Galatians in this book. We will focus on the theological themes that serve as the foundation of—and offer a defense for—the beliefs and doctrines held by mainstream Christianity today.[2] Why do Christians believe what we believe? How do we distinguish the true gospel of Jesus from false gospels? This epistle has played a significant part in addressing such issues throughout church history.

Galatians so influenced the reformer Martin Luther that it is the only book of the Bible on which he wrote two separate commentaries. And it played an explosive role in the most significant doctrinal debate of the past millennium. Paul's discussion of justification by faith alone in Galatians 2–3 is the dynamite that rocked the foundation of the Christian church in the sixteenth century, leading to the Reformation. This epistle (along with its big brother, Romans) was instrumental to the doctrine of *sola fide* (faith alone), which Luther considered the issue on which the church would stand or fall.

In contemporary Christendom, apologist Myles Christian has referred to the epistle of Galatians as the "red pill" of Seventh-Day Adventism (SDA). Paul's arguments against a different gospel (1:6–9) have served as a powerful antidote to the limited "present truth" gospel and other unbiblical ideas espoused in SDA theology. This letter has played a significant role in breaking the spell of Seventh-Day Adventism and bringing many to a spiritual epiphany about the true gospel and their freedom in Christ.

Paul passionately argues against the false teachers infiltrating the churches he had planted in Galatia. These were Jewish believers in Jesus who taught that Gentile believers were required to be circumcised and keep the law of Moses in order to follow Him. The Bible often refers to them as the "circumcision party."[3] Scholars use the term *Judaizers*, which comes from a Greek verb coined by the apostle Paul: *ioudaizō*.[4] He uses this verb in Galatians 2:14 to mean "live like Jews."

Because of humanity's ever-present struggle with antisemitism, I am compelled to issue a warning to the reader. As a Jewish man, Paul had no problem with believers voluntarily living according to Jewish customs (1 Cor. 9:19–23). The problem arose when those traditions were taught as a *requirement* for following Jesus. While there is nothing wrong with the term *Judaizer* in itself, it would be a grave error to read the concept of anti-Jewishness or antisemitism into it. As Bible-believing Christians, we have to acknowledge that Jesus was born a Jewish man under the Jewish law (4:4–5). He is the Jewish Messiah promised in the Hebrew Scriptures[5] who taught "Salvation is from the Jews" (John 4:22).

In other words, the gospel of Jesus is a Jewish story that features Jewish good guys and Jewish bad guys. And in Galatians, we will see that some first-century Jews mistakenly thought Gentiles needed to live like Jews in order to follow the Jewish Messiah. This is not an indictment against all Jewish people. In fact, as we will explore, given the theological revolution they were experiencing during the first days of God's new covenant, the Judaizers' confusion on this issue was understandable.

Far less defendable is the modern-day version of "Judaizing" taught by theologies like *Torahism*, which you may know as Hebrew Roots or Torah-observant Christianity. These radical movements (made up entirely of Gentiles, ironically) teach the same thing the circumcision party taught in the first century, namely, that followers of Jesus are required to keep the old covenant law. This rigid legalism is also found in some sects of fundamentalist Christianity which, despite having better theology, preach works righteousness and over-emphasize stringent conformity to moral codes. In Galatians, Paul mounts a powerful defense against such a hairsplitting approach to our faith.

Paul also addresses errors on the opposite end of the theological spectrum. In preaching freedom in Christ, the apostle is quick to add, "Do not use your freedom to indulge the flesh; rather, serve one another humbly in love" (5:13). The abuse of Christian freedom is most evident in the self-focused pseudo-spiritualism of ideologies like progressive Christianity, the prosperity gospel, and the Word of Faith movement. These theologies want to maintain a connection to God without submitting to His authority. Spirituality is used as a means to serve fleshly desires in the form of material wealth, moral autonomy, and sexual freedom.

Theologians call such errors *antinomianism*, which means against (*anti*) law (*nomos*). It is the false idea that, since faith is the only thing required for salvation, believers are free from even the moral obligations of the law. Rather than submitting to the authority of the Word of God, these belief systems try to mold the Bible to fit the shape of prevailing cultural norms. This kind of thinking celebrates ideas like following one's own heart and deserving our best life now while ignoring the teachings of Jesus about dying to self, taking up our cross, and serving others.

Paul's teaching that Christians are no longer under the law is sometimes misunderstood as antinomian. The apostle, however, speaks out against such lawlessness. In Galatians, the apostle does a masterful job of articulating a proper biblical balance between our glorious freedom in Jesus and our ongoing obligation of obedience and submission to God. Indeed, as we will see, Paul warns about ditches on both sides of the road: legalism and antinomianism.

One last thing before we move on to an overview of Galatians. It's important to remember that Paul wrote this text as a letter. It was intended to be read in one sitting and understood as a whole. In this book, we will carefully and methodically work our way through the text verse by verse, and I believe you will find this a fascinating and profitable journey. However, before you dive into our study, I would encourage you to take fifteen minutes and read through the book of Galatians for yourself in one sitting. This will give you a better understanding of the flow of Paul's thoughts, the state of his heart, and the range of topics being discussed.

THE SHAPE AND SETTING
OF GALATIANS

The original NT text did not include chapter or verse numbers.[1] So, as we work through the text of Galatians, our journey will be guided by the contours of thought more than verse and chapter numbers. While the entire letter is a sustained argument against the false teachings of the Judaizers, it is loosely made up of three sections. You won't see these sections labeled in your Bible, of course. But they serve as a helpful guide to the flow of Paul's thoughts.

Chapters 1–2 are largely historical. Here, Paul is a church historian providing the backstory of the communities of faith in Galatia, the early mission of the church, and his own autobiography. This is the only place in the Bible that reveals what happened to the apostle after his encounter with the resurrected Jesus on the road to Damascus (Acts 9:1–19). We also learn how Paul was taught the gospel, where he got his apostolic authority, and how the other apostles in Jerusalem accepted him when they first met.

Chapters 3–4 are predominantly theological. Here, Paul is a theology professor mounting a masterful argument against the false teachers in Galatia based almost entirely on the Old Testament (OT). He repeatedly points his readers back to Abraham and the history of Israel to teach them about Christ. In this section, Paul connects many dots between the OT and the gospel of Jesus. He artfully walks us through profound theological and intertextual themes, linking together the law, the Christ, and the promise.

The final section, chapters 5–6, are pastoral. Here, Paul is a concerned pastor focusing on the real-world application of his arguments. He explains how believers should live based on the truths he has shared and what it means to be free in Christ and walk by the Spirit. This section includes the famous list of the fruit of the Spirit (5:22–23). We also find two rare and fascinating phrases in this section: "law of Christ" (6:2)[2] and "Israel of God" (6:16).[3]

Historical-Cultural Setting

I'll be honest. Understanding the *who, when, where,* and *why* behind this text isn't technically necessary to appreciate the basic message of Galatians. However, doing so unlocks many hidden gems for us. It's the difference between looking at a photo of the *Mona Lisa* and stepping into the Louvre Museum in Paris to see the brushstrokes and colors in real life. There is a richness and depth that comes into view when we understand the historical and cultural setting in which Paul wrote this letter. While it wasn't written *to* contemporary believers, it was definitely written *for* us. God knew His church would desperately need the wisdom found in this epistle.

The majority of evidence for our understanding of Galatians comes from the letter itself. From the text, we can develop a picture of the author, the recipients, the date, and the occasion for writing. This picture can be further developed with details found in other NT books, especially Acts, Romans, and 1–2 Corinthians. In fact, a number of theological concepts that are discussed briefly and densely in Galatians are later filled out and elaborated on in Paul's letter to the Romans. So, we'll occasionally jump over to those other biblical texts to add detail and color to the apostle's letter to the Galatians. Let's take a brief look at the basics.

Literary genre and author. Galatians is an *epistle*, a form of personal correspondence. Rather than a broad treatise on God, this is a deeply pastoral and profoundly theological letter written to address a specific issue with a particular audience. Paul's authorship is roundly accepted, even among skeptical scholars. He identifies himself in the opening words as "Paul,[4] an apostle" (1:1) and later writes, "I, Paul, tell you . . ." (5:2). Notably, he mentions writing from within a community of believers. The opening "from" statement says, "Paul, an apostle . . . and all the brothers and sisters with me" (1:1–2). It's not clear why he mentions others in his greeting. Perhaps he wrote this personal letter with the support of a church community.[5] If that is the case, it would be unique among all of the apostle's writings.

Figure 1: Map of Galatia showing the northern and southern regions.

Recipients and geography. Galatians is expressly addressed "to the churches in Galatia" (1:2). Paul is not writing to an individual (as with his letters to Timothy, Titus, and Philemon), but rather to a collection of Christian communities located in an area he calls "Galatia." The specific region he references is a matter of debate. There are two possibilities, both located in modern-day Turkey. In the first century, the name "Galatia" was used to refer to a loose geographic area in the north settled by an Indo-European people known as the Gauls.[6] The same name was also used to refer to a Roman province in the south. Because of this, scholars have developed two primary theories about Paul's intended audience, which are referred to by the rather unimaginative labels "North Galatians Theory" and "South Galatians Theory."

While we can't know with certainty which area Paul was targeting based on the text of the NT, I believe southern Galatia is the more likely option. The book of Acts reveals that Paul visited many cities in South Galatia on his missionary journeys, including Derbe, Lystra, Iconium, and "Pisidian" Antioch. There are several additional details in the text of Galatians that support the South Galatians theory. The good news is that while the particular region is of great historical interest, it does not ultimately affect the apostle's theological teachings or their influence on Christian doctrine.

Date of composition. Like the location of the Galatians, the date of composition of the letter is also a matter of debate. The discussion primarily focuses on the text in Galatians 2:1–10, where Paul describes meeting with church leaders in Jerusalem. Could he be referring to the same meeting Luke recorded in Acts 15:1–29, known as the Jerusalem Council? Acts 15 describes a sharp dispute between Paul and the circumcision party that occurred around 50 CE. Because Paul participated in that council and addressed very similar issues in Galatians, some scholars see Acts 15 and Galatians 2 as referring to the same event. Therefore, they date the writing of Galatians to 54–55 CE.

Others conclude, and I agree, that despite the similar topic, there are too many gaps for Galatians 2 to be describing the Acts 15 Jerusalem Council. Moreover, Galatians contains no reference to the council's decision, which would have been highly significant given the letter's subject matter. So, I take the view that Galatians is Paul's earliest writing and can be dated to 48–49 CE, just before the Jerusalem Council. Of course, the debated window of time is relatively narrow, historically speaking, and knowing the exact date doesn't necessarily affect our understanding of the letter. But it does add color to our discussion and helps trace the thoughts of the apostle Paul chronologically through his NT writings.

Occasion. What prompted Paul to compose the text of Galatians, and what did he hope to achieve by writing it? The text reveals he was writing to faith communities he had visited (and likely founded) in Galatia, who were "turning to a different gospel—which is really no gospel at all" (1:6–7). False teachers had infiltrated their ranks and begun to lead the Galatian believers astray. "Evidently some people are throwing you into confusion and are trying to pervert the gospel of Christ" (1:7). Paul had somehow heard grave news about his beloved churches in Galatia and penned a passionate pastoral letter to warn them and provide guidance and instruction.

Unfortunately, the text does not explicitly describe the false ideas in question. Paul knew what they were, of course, as did his recipients. However, because this was a personal letter, the apostle felt no need to list them in detail. Reading Galatians is a little like sitting beside someone talking on the phone. We only hear one side of the conversation, so we have to piece together what the other side is saying based on the bits we can hear.

Thankfully, there are a lot of clues in Galatians, which we will look at in detail as we work our way through the text. We will learn that the false teachers were Jewish believers in Jesus who taught that Gentiles were required to be circumcised and keep the law of Moses in order to follow Christ. In fact, let's take a moment to consider both the historical setting in which Paul wrote this letter and why the false teachers took such a position. Knowing the wider historical background really helps the text come alive.

A Unique Time in History

In the sport of track and field, there is an event called a *relay race* in which team members take turns running around a track while carrying a baton. When the first runner completes her leg of the race, she hands off the baton to the next runner. By rule, this handoff must occur within a small section of the track known as the *crossover box*. So, for a brief time during a race, a team has two runners on the track at the same time. The first runner is completing her leg as the next runner picks up speed and takes off.

Likewise, the forty-year historical period between the resurrection of Christ and the destruction of the Jerusalem temple (30–70 CE) can be thought of as a "crossover box" for the old and new covenants. God's people were in a liminal state. The physical temple and Levitical priesthood were still operational (though about to end) even as new believers in Jesus—whom the NT calls a temple and a priesthood[7]—were getting up to speed. This was a time of confusion and transformation. In fact, the changes introduced under the new covenant were so profound that the church ultimately took centuries to fully understand what they entailed.

We look back on this transitional period through the lens of twenty centuries of historical processing and with the advantage of a body of inspired texts called the New Testament. The first-century believers in Galatia had neither; they were living these events in real time. Keep this historical perspective in mind as we work through Paul's letter. To fully grasp his theological arguments, we need to understand how the original recipients in Galatia would have viewed the claims of the Judaizers in light of the gospel that Paul had taught them.

The writings of the NT present a first-century story in roughly chronological order, and it's important to recognize where the book of Galatians fits into that timeline. Matthew, Mark, Luke, and John are essentially historical biographies of Jesus covering the period from just before His birth until right after His resurrection. The rest of the NT covers the years immediately following the resurrection. Said another way, the gospels reveal Jesus and what He taught, while the rest of the NT reveals what His life and ministry means for the world.

Galatians, Hebrews, Romans, and other epistles were written during this post-resurrection "crossover" period when Jews and Gentiles alike were trying to work out what the death and resurrection of Jesus meant for them. The gospel was starting to spread, and Christ's new church was emerging. As part of this process, Jesus personally called Paul[8] and, through him, provided His bride, the church, with a theological framework for understanding what faith in Him meant. Indeed, much of what Paul wrote, including this letter to the Galatians, was intended to provide clarity and guidance to the nascent church as it wrestled to gain its bearings in the first years of the new covenant era.

"Scripture" for first-century believers consisted only of what we now call the Old Testament. This is the same body of text our Jewish friends call the Hebrew Bible, or the *Tanakh*.[9] Jesus taught that the Hebrew Bible pointed to Him. "Everything must be fulfilled that is written about me in the Law of Moses, the Prophets and the Psalms" (Luke 24:44). For thousands of years, God had been directing and shaping human history and providing clues that pointed to His future Messiah. Jesus, of course, was that promised Messiah. In fact, the English word *Christ* essentially means "Messiah."[10]

By the time Paul wrote his letter to the Galatians, Jesus had already appeared and walked among us. He had been crucified and resurrected, and then ascended to heaven. These events happened less than twenty years before Paul penned this epistle. Some still living had heard Jesus preach and even met Him in person. Thus, the believers in Galatia were dealing with a very recent theological development.

When Jesus, as God incarnate, arrived on the timeline of human history, a theological bomb exploded. The life of Christ split history in two, dividing our calendars into the Before Common Era years and the Common Era years. (Or, as I refer to it, the "Christ Era.") Jesus inaugurated the new covenant that God had promised to Jeremiah over 600 years earlier (Jer. 31:31–34), introducing a different and, in many ways, surprising new arrangement between God and His people.

Paul's letter to the Galatians was written in the immediate aftermath of this "explosion." Theologically speaking, believers were still reeling and confused; dust and debris were everywhere. Consequently, Paul and the other NT authors wrote letters (under the supervision of the Holy Spirit) intended to bring order to the theological chaos of Christ's brand-new church. Scholar Moisés Silva provides helpful insight:

> The letter to the Galatians deals directly with the most basic theological question faced by the first Christian generation: How does the gospel of Jesus Christ affect the Jewish/Gentile division? The first Christians were Jewish, and at the beginning it was assumed by them that the special character of their nation, and thus the ceremonial observances related to it, would be continued. When Gentiles began to receive the gospel in significant numbers, those assumptions were challenged, and it took a prolonged period of reflection, adjustment and struggle to understand God's purposes for Jew and Gentile.[11]

Today, it's easy to see that Jesus inaugurated a new covenant and ushered in a whole new way for God's people to relate to Him.

But at the time Galatians was written, these things were not so clear. There was no mass media announcement, no email campaign, no newsletter with talking points to quickly get everyone up to speed. For Gentile believers, following Jesus was an entirely novel enterprise with no real analog to the polytheistic, pagan world they knew. Jewish believers, on the other hand, faced a more daunting challenge.

Christianity emerged out of first-century Jewish faith and culture. The first believers in Jesus were Jews. Jesus's Hebrew name is *Yeshua*—which literally means "salvation"—and He taught that "salvation is from the Jews" (John 4:22). Following Jesus was initially known simply as "the Way,"[12] and it was considered a Jewish movement. Yet Jewish believers in Jesus were forced to wrestle with a paradigm shift of biblical proportions. Here was their promised Messiah, foretold in the Hebrew Scriptures, dedicated in the temple in Jerusalem (Luke 2:22–23), and "born under the law" (4:4). Surely, anyone who wanted to follow Him would need to convert to Judaism by being circumcised and keeping the Jewish law, right?

Many early Jewish believers in Jesus understandably (yet mistakenly) argued that these obligations should be required of Gentiles who came to faith. Theologian Mark Keown writes:

> The first Jewish Christians did not initially grasp what Jesus meant and that God had to move sovereignly to cause them to realize the cosmic scope of mission . . . They struggled to understand how the gospel could reach Gentiles without them having to come under the Mosaic law to receive God's blessing . . . It seems that the first Christians remained locked into a Jewish mindset concerning the salvation of the gentiles: they believed gentiles would be saved by . . . becoming Jews through being circumcised and following Christ in the context of Judaism. They failed to grasp the truly gracious and cosmic nature of God's mission—that they were sent to go to the world with a

gospel of grace without the requirement of circumcision and submission to Mosaic law.[13]

This was perhaps the most controversial issue in the first-century Christian world. How could Gentile believers be allowed into the family of Yahweh, the God of Israel, without having to keep the Jewish law? Paul's letter to the Galatians is the earliest NT text to directly address this issue. Acts 15 reveals this was such a hot-button issue that it prompted the first known church council in history.

The Jerusalem Council is dated to 50 CE, less than twenty years after the resurrection and only a year or two after Galatians was written. In attendance were a "who's who" of the early church: Paul, Peter, James, Barnabas, and other apostles and elders. They gathered in Jerusalem, debated the issue, and ultimately determined that Gentile believers were not required to be circumcised or keep the law of Moses. Instead, because the Council knew that Gentiles would be living, eating, and doing life with their new Jewish brothers and sisters in Christ, it gave them just a few restrictions intended to foster unity in the emerging church (Acts 15:28–29).

There is one further issue worth considering before we turn to the text of Galatians. Why did God include this book in the canon of Scripture? I believe at least one reason is because He knew that the false teachings Paul dismantles in this letter would reappear in various forms over the centuries. The body of Christ would need biblical counsel and direction to navigate these issues. And when it comes to modern apologetics, Galatians is a fervent *tour de force*. In fact, it is unique among Paul's writings because of its fiery tone. The nineteenth-century French professor Auguste Sabatier captures it well:

> The style does not sustain the thought; it is the thought which
> sustains the style, giving to it its force, its life, its beauty. Thought

presses on, overcharged, breathless and hurried, dragging the words after it. . . . Unfinished phrases, daring omissions, parentheses which leave us out of sight and out of breath, rabbinical subtleties, audacious paradoxes, vehement apostrophes—pour in like surging billows. Mere words in their ordinary meaning are insufficient to sustain this overwhelming plenitude of thought and feeling.[14]

In other words, as we will see, Paul is worked up. He is heartbroken and angry. There is a sense of urgency and heightened emotion in the apostle's words, revealing the importance he attached to the issues he was addressing. This instancy is evident from the opening lines of his letter.

Part I

PAUL, THE CHURCH HISTORIAN

CALLED BY GOD

Galatians 1:1–24

❧

Given the background we've just discussed, let's step into the sandals of a first-century believer in Galatia. The first thing to remember is that there were no printing presses or a public postal system. Copies of Paul's epistle were made by hand, one pen stroke at a time. A network of rank-and-file believers invested significant human and financial resources in distributing these texts among the churches.

Early Christianity was an unusually "bookish" religion. Historian Larry Hurtado notes:

> Reading, writing, copying, and dissemination of texts had a major place—indeed, a prominence—in early Christianity that . . . was unusual for religious groups of the Roman era.[1]

Professor Harry Gamble describes "a busy, almost hectic traffic of messengers and letters between the churches" of Asia Minor.[2] Early Christians inherently thought of themselves as connected with other believers in different locations and felt it vital to share the letters of the apostles with one another. From the earliest days, those texts were considered authoritative and treated with great reverence.

We don't know how many copies of this epistle Paul originally had delivered to Galatia, but we can imagine how eagerly his letter would have been received. The news surely spread like wildfire throughout the community. *Did you hear? A letter arrived from the apostle Paul!* Because of the cost of copying texts and low literacy rates, reading privately was a rare affair in the first century. This was an oral culture. So, the believers in Galatia would have gathered in a private home or a synagogue to hear Paul's words read aloud. This allowed the entire community to receive his teachings and instructions at the same time.

The reader selected from among the community in Galatia wouldn't have been merely literate. He would have been able to articulate Paul's words clearly and accurately: probably a church leader or elder. Let's step into that warm and dusty assembly in Galatia and take a seat in the corner. The crowd is murmuring. The church leader stands, Paul's letter in hand. A hush comes over the room. The orator clears his throat and begins reading aloud to the faithful and curious alike.

> [1]Paul, an apostle—sent not from men nor by a man, but by Jesus Christ and God the Father, who raised him from the dead—[2]and all the brothers and sisters with me,
>
> To the churches in Galatia.

Surely, these words were met with warm smiles and nods. Many in attendance had met Paul on his previous trip to the area, which had occurred as little as three years before the arrival of this letter. This is their spiritual mentor writing to his beloved brothers and sisters in Christ. Many in the room had come to faith because of Paul, and the very mention of his name brought his face and voice to mind.

Like Paul's other letters, Galatians begins with a salutation that follows the typical format of the time; author followed by addressees. From the very first line, Paul begins defending the authenticity of his apostleship. He is not an apostle sent by men "but by Jesus Christ and God the Father" (1:1). This issue is at the top of his mind. His authority will play a major role in his argument with the Judaizers. The false teachers in Galatia were trying to cast Paul as a rogue preacher out of step with the "real" apostles, who had actually walked with Jesus before His crucifixion. But Paul argues from the opening sentence that, in fact, his apostolic status was conferred by Jesus Himself.

The Greek term *apostolos* ("one who is sent, messenger") is a military term that describes someone sent on a mission under the authority of a person of a higher rank. Think of a general sending one of his officers out as a delegate or envoy. That officer carries the authority of the general. For instance, when Jesus sent out the seventy-two messengers, He told them, "Whoever listens to you listens to me; whoever rejects you rejects me; but whoever rejects me rejects him who sent me" (Luke 10:16). To reject the Son sent by God is to reject God Himself. Likewise, to reject an apostle sent by Jesus is to deny Jesus Himself. Paul is warning both the Galatians and the false teachers among them that if they reject his teachings, they are rejecting Jesus Himself, who had said of Paul, "This man is my chosen instrument to proclaim my name to the Gentiles and their kings and to the people of Israel" (Acts 9:15).

Believe it or not, the apostle's warning equally applies to various "law-keeping" movements in Christianity today. Rather than accepting the words of Paul as authoritative, they marginalize or even reject his writings because they do not fit their theology. To paraphrase Augustine, if you believe what you like in the Bible and reject what you don't, it is not the Bible you believe but yourself.

Paul continues,

> ³Grace and peace to you from God our Father and the Lord Jesus Christ, ⁴who gave himself for our sins to rescue us from

> the present evil age, according to the will of our God and
> Father, ⁵to whom be glory for ever and ever. Amen.

More smiles and nods. At this point in his opening salutation, Paul will typically include a statement of thanksgiving and praise. Consider the warm sentiments expressed at this point in some of his other letters:

I thank my God through Jesus Christ for all of you, because your faith is being reported all over the world. (Rom. 1:8)

I always thank my God for you because of his grace given you in Christ Jesus. (1 Cor. 1:4)

We always thank God, the Father of our Lord Jesus Christ, when we pray for you. (Col. 1:3)

We always thank God for all of you and continually mention you in our prayers. (1 Thess. 1:2)

There will be neither thanksgiving nor praise for the Galatians. This is our first clue that something is amiss. Rather than offering a warm statement of gratitude, Paul abruptly shifts gears and begins admonishing the Galatian believers in exasperation. He has heard disturbing news and means to get to the bottom of it:

> ⁶I am astonished that you are so quickly deserting the one
> who called you to live in the grace of Christ and are turning to
> a different gospel—⁷which is really no gospel at all. Evidently
> some people are throwing you into confusion and are trying
> to pervert the gospel of Christ. ⁸But even if we or an angel
> from heaven should preach a gospel other than the one we
> preached to you, let them be under God's curse! ⁹As we have

> already said, so now I say again: If anybody is preaching to you a gospel other than what you accepted, let them be under God's curse!

Paul is writing with intense emotion. If he was dictating this letter to an *amanuensis* (a literary assistant), it's easy to imagine him pacing back and forth, gesturing excitedly as the scribe hurriedly reinks his quill, trying to keep up. Paul knows these people. He had preached the gospel to them and was instrumental in founding their churches. He is worried about his beloved Galatians because "some people are throwing you into confusion and are trying to pervert the gospel of Christ" (1:7).

This epistle contains arguably the most direct and forceful language in the NT. Paul's harshest remarks are not leveled at pagans persecuting the church from the outside but at those leading believers astray from the inside. His approach is modeled on Jesus, who was patient and longsuffering with outsiders like prostitutes, tax collectors, and the general public. Jesus's harshest rebukes were reserved for insiders—especially leaders like the Pharisees and teachers of the law—who were leading people astray. Paul knew—as Jesus had known—that, going all the way back to the golden calf at Sinai, the greatest threat to God's family is not from the outside but from the inside.

A Closer Look at the Golden Calf

The incident of the golden calf recorded in Exodus 32 is not just notable because the Israelites bowed down and worshipped an idol, but that the idea arose from within the faith community. They weren't led astray by false teachers from the outside. The idea to create an idol and worship it came from the very people who had heard God forbid such things with their own ears.[3]

In the shadow of Mount Sinai, just days after Moses had ascended the mountain to meet with Yahweh, the people gathered around Aaron, who had recently been appointed high priest, and said, "Come, make us gods who will go before us" (Exod. 32:1). And Aaron did so! Not only did he melt down gold and shape it into a calf, but he also built an altar in front of it. Then he announced, "Tomorrow there will be a festival to the LORD" (Exod. 32:5). What? How can you hold a feast to Yahweh with an idol of a golden calf?

What seems obvious in hindsight was not so apparent to the Israelites in the moment. (Isn't that how sin always works?) They were fresh out of centuries of slavery in the pagan nation of Egypt. Ancient Near Eastern iconography reveals that bulls and calves were commonly pictured as the pedestal on which a deity stood. Maybe the Israelites felt that they were giving Yahweh an exalted place to dwell by making a golden calf. However, Yahweh had already told them that He would dwell among them in the tabernacle.[4] Apparently, the Israelites thought they had a better idea. And, what's worse, they were worshipping the idol itself. The Israelites needed someone in their midst (an apologist, perhaps!) to stand up and declare, "This is not what God said!"

In terms of apologetics, the belief systems that pose the biggest threat to the body of Christ are not Islam, atheism, Buddhism, or any other "ism" that openly rejects Jesus. Those are skirmishes with easily identifiable opponents across clearly marked battle lines. The far more dangerous threat comes from people wearing the same uniform as you and carrying the same flag but following a different battle plan. Their damage is inflicted through unexpected friendly fire. These are the people Paul describes as teaching "a different gospel—which is really no gospel at all" (1:6–7).

Counterfeit gospels presented an existential threat to the first-century church, and that threat remains to this day. Paul staunchly declared that there is no different gospel and no second gospel. Even if an "angel from heaven" (1:8) tries to tell you otherwise, there is only one gospel of Christ. This is the ever-present question the church must ask itself: Are we still committed to the one true gospel of Jesus? Or have we veered off course a bit and begun mixing in other ideas? Thankfully, it is never too late to make course corrections.

In modern history, we've encountered movements like *theological liberalism*, which views Christianity as a religion of social reconstruction. Theologian Gary Dorrien notes that liberalism does not recognize an external authority in Christianity. Rather, it believes religion "should be modern and progressive and that the meaning of Christianity should be interpreted from the standpoint of modern knowledge and experience."[5] This perspective has encouraged thinkers like Rudolf Bultmann, who sought to "demythologize" the gospels by stripping away their outdated and undesirable worldview so that they could be understood in a modern context. More recently, we find a "gospel of inclusion" preached by progressive Christianity, in which inclusion of "sexual others" is exalted as the highest moral value, even if what is being included directly contradicts God's Word. These kinds of "Christian" movements do not deny Christ or oppose the gospel outright but rather seek to reshape it from within.

This is what the apostle Paul saw happening in first-century Galatia. He describes the false teachers as "trying to pervert the gospel of Christ" (1:7). And he doesn't merely demand they be rebuked or silenced. He twice repeats, "Let them be under God's curse!" (1:8, 9). The Greek word is *anathema*. This heavy-duty term carries the idea of being banned or even devoted to the Lord for destruction. As a well-read Jewish man, Paul knew full well that the ancient nation of Israel did not ultimately fall because of external enemies. The root cause was the infighting, disobedience, and disloyalty of the Israelites themselves. As God declared through the prophet Jeremiah, "They broke my covenant, though I was a husband to them" (Jer. 31:32). Accordingly, Paul knew the grave danger of divergent internal influences.

Who are these false teachers in Galatia? What were they teaching? Unfortunately, Paul doesn't answer either question in detail. Nevertheless, we will be able to piece together a decent picture from the text as we go. So far, we know that the issue at the top of his mind—indeed, the reason he penned this letter—is that false teachers in Galatia had begun influencing the believers and endangering the gospel. We've already seen a couple clues as to the specifics of their teaching.

Paul accuses the Galatians of turning to "a different gospel" (1:6) and declares that the false teachers are attempting to "pervert the gospel of Christ" (1:7). The Greek word behind *pervert* is *metastrepho*, which means "to change, alter, or distort." This tells us that the problem isn't a corrupting influence from the pagan world. Rather, it is a distortion of the gospel of Jesus Christ, the Jewish Messiah. Teachers among the Galatians are preaching something that resembles the true gospel but has been distorted or perverted to an alarming degree. Paul is astonished the Galatians could have fallen for such a counterfeit gospel. You have to wonder if some of those false teachers were sitting in the crowd listening to Paul's letter being read aloud. If so, they were squirming in their seats.

The most insidious false teachings are those that closely resemble the truth. Absurd theology sticks out like *Monopoly* money in a pile of U.S. currency. Conversely, teachings only off by a few degrees are much less likely to trip an alarm. These kinds of doctrines lead the most Christians astray. This is as true today as it was in first-century Galatia. It is why we need to regularly read and study our Bibles. You don't need to be a professional theologian to detect when something isn't quite right. If you're familiar enough with the genuine article, counterfeit gospels will catch your eye.

The teachings of the Judaizers in Galatia were a convincing counterfeit bill. This is why their theology was accepted as plausible by many believers in Galatians who had been discipled by the apostle Paul himself. This is the "danger from within" he was contending against. Early Christians were especially susceptible to plausible heresies since they did not have the advantage of a NT. They were *living* the NT. Remember, the Galatians were trying to work out their faith in the theological aftermath of Jesus's resurrection. They found themselves in a "he said / they said" situation: Paul said one thing, the false teachers said another. Whom should they believe?

One way the Judaizers tried to convince the Galatians of the superiority of their doctrine was by undermining Paul's authority. *Who is this guy, Paul, anyway? He's not a real apostle; he wasn't sent out by the Jerusalem church.* Paul responds:

> [10]Am I now trying to win the approval of human beings, or of God? Or am I trying to please people? If I were still trying to please people, I would not be a servant of Christ.

Because Paul was an apostle to the Gentiles,[6] the Judaizers accused him of watering down the Torah to make his gospel more appealing and win their approval. He flatly denies this charge. In fact, Paul will later reveal that his commitment to the purity of the gospel of Jesus is the source of persecution in his life (5:11). If his goal was to please men, he would certainly not be a *servant* of Christ. The Greek word is *doulos*, which literally means "slave." This term foreshadows a central theme that will soon emerge.

Paul then begins to share a personal testimony to underscore his God-given authority:

> [11] I want you to know, brothers and sisters, that the gospel I preached is not of human origin. [12] I did not receive it from any man, nor was I taught it; rather, I received it by revelation from Jesus Christ.

Paul's dramatic conversion on a road outside Damascus is recorded in Acts 9:1–19. One minute, Paul was a Jewish zealot "breathing out murderous threats against the Lord's disciples" (Acts 9:1). The next moment, he was on his back, knocked to the ground by a light from heaven. The voice of Jesus thundered, "Saul, Saul, why do you persecute me?" (Acts 9:4). The Lord commanded him to get up and go into the city, and Paul was struck blind. Jesus then declared to a disciple named Ananias that Paul "is my chosen instrument to proclaim my name to the Gentiles and their kings and to the people of Israel. I will show him how much he must suffer for my name" (Acts 9:15–16). Jesus thus sent Paul as His *apostolos*.

After three days of blindness, Ananias touched Paul's eyes, his sight was restored, and he was baptized as a believer in Jesus (Acts 9:17–19). Saul, the Jewish man who had been violently persecuting Christians, had become a Christian who would be violently persecuted by some of his fellow Jews because of that same faith. After Paul's conversion, who taught him the gospel? He reveals, "I received it by revelation from Jesus Christ" (1:12). The idea that no one sat the newly converted apostle down and explained the gospel to him is incredible. Thirteen of the NT's twenty-seven books came from Paul's pen. They are instrumental in defining the theological framework of the Christian faith.

God equips those whom He calls. The Bible contains example after example of God passing over the most impressive and qualified of candidates and choosing instead to use the weak and unlikely—reluctant Moses, cowardly Gideon, rebellious Jonah. In Paul, we see Jesus appointing the most outspoken adversary of His church as His chosen instrument to grow that church (Acts 9:15). You have to wonder if Paul had his own unlikely calling in mind when he penned these hopeful words to the believers in Corinth:

> Brothers and sisters, think of what you were when you were called. Not many of you were wise by human standards; not many were influential; not many were of noble birth. But God chose the foolish things of the world to shame the wise; God chose the weak things of the world to shame the strong. God chose the lowly things of this world and the despised things—and the things that are not—to nullify the things that are, so that no one may boast before him. (1 Cor. 1:26–29)

Understanding that Paul's letter to the Galatians is an apologetic against false teachers helps explain why he specifically points out that he did not receive the gospel from any man but from Christ Himself (1:12). After Paul planted the churches in Galatia, the Judaizers showed up and tried to throw him under the bus. They wanted to discredit Paul's message by painting him as an itinerant preacher with no real credentials. Paul responds to those accusations by informing the Galatians that he learned the gospel directly from Jesus, just like the other apostles.

His testimony continues:

> [13]For you have heard of my previous way of life in Judaism, how intensely I persecuted the church of God and tried to destroy it. [14]I was advancing in Judaism beyond many of my own age among my people and was extremely zealous for the traditions of my fathers. [15]But when God, who set me apart from my mother's womb and called me by his grace,

> was pleased [16]to reveal his Son in me so that I might preach him among the Gentiles, my immediate response was not to consult any human being. [17]I did not go up to Jerusalem to see those who were apostles before I was, but I went into Arabia. Later I returned to Damascus.

My faith is continually strengthened when I realize how grounded Christianity is in the timeline of human history. Unlike the myths and the texts of other religions, Judeo-Christian writings are filled with the names of real historical people, cities, rulers, and events. This makes them falsifiable, which, in turn, gives the text of our faith the weight and feel of reality. These aren't whimsical ancient legends made up by Bronze Era barbarians, as many atheists claim. Rather, the Bible tells the story of real human history and a real, living God.

After Paul's conversion, he didn't consult anyone. He didn't go up to Jerusalem to see the apostles and immediately make his mission known. Instead, he went to the land east and south of ancient Palestine (which would be present-day Saudi Arabia). After an unspecified amount of time, Paul returned to Damascus and spent three years there. By sharing these details, he may be implying that he studied with Jesus for three years before officially beginning his ministry on his own, just like the other apostles had done. Paul wants his readers to understand that he is every bit a real apostle of Jesus.

Paul doesn't provide much detail about his time in Damascus. Thankfully, Luke fills in some gaps for us in Acts 9:

> Saul spent several days with the disciples in Damascus. At once he began to preach in the synagogues that Jesus is the Son of God. All those who heard him were astonished and asked, "Isn't he the man who raised havoc in Jerusalem among those who call on this name? And hasn't he come here to take them as prisoners

to the chief priests?" Yet Saul grew more and more powerful and baffled the Jews living in Damascus by proving that Jesus is the Messiah.

After many days had gone by, there was a conspiracy among the Jews to kill him, but Saul learned of their plan. Day and night they kept close watch on the city gates in order to kill him. But his followers took him by night and lowered him in a basket through an opening in the wall. (Acts 9:19–25)

Luke reports that Paul "grew more and more powerful and baffled the Jews living in Damascus by proving that Jesus is the Messiah" (Acts 9:22). The three years he spent there seemed to serve as a training period in which he poured over the Hebrew Scriptures under the guidance of the Holy Spirit and let his theology catch up with what his heart and soul had experienced on that road outside of Damascus.

Back in Galatians 1, Paul continues his story. He recounts his journey to Jerusalem to visit with the apostle Peter, whose Aramaic name was Cephas:

> 18Then after three years, I went up to Jerusalem to get acquainted with Cephas and stayed with him fifteen days. 19I saw none of the other apostles—only James, the Lord's brother. 20I assure you before God that what I am writing you is no lie.

By the time Paul finally met Peter in Jerusalem, he would have been a mature believer with a thorough grasp of the gospel and experience preaching it. As the de facto leader of the nascent church, Peter was the most well-known apostle at the time. Paul uses the Greek word *historēsai* to describe his meeting with Peter; it means "get acquainted with" or "make the acquaintance of." This may have been their first face-to-face meeting, although they had likely been aware of one another by reputation. Former foes meeting as allies for the first time makes for an apprehensive gathering! Acts 9 provides a glimpse into how Paul was received:

> When [Paul] came to Jerusalem, he tried to join the disciples, but they were all afraid of him, not believing that he really was a disciple. But Barnabas took him and brought him to the apostles. He told them how Saul on his journey had seen the Lord and that the Lord had spoken to him, and how in Damascus he had preached fearlessly in the name of Jesus. So Saul stayed with them and moved about freely in Jerusalem, speaking boldly in the name of the Lord. (Acts 9:26–28)

Barnabas had to step in and vouch for Paul, informing the disciples in Jerusalem of his dramatic conversion and how it had led to an authentic life change. Paul describes the visit as short, lasting just fifteen days. He visited Peter and met Jesus's brother, James, who allowed him to move freely in Jerusalem and preach in the name of Jesus. This is highly significant; Paul shares these details to add to his credibility as an apostle. He wants the Galatians to know that he was accepted by the other apostles in Jerusalem. They approved of his theology and let him preach in the name of the Lord.

Paul's testimony continues:

> 21Then I went to Syria and Cilicia. 22I was personally unknown to the churches of Judea that are in Christ. 23They only heard the report: "The man who formerly persecuted us is now preaching the faith he once tried to destroy." 24And they praised God because of me.

Although Paul wasn't yet well known as an apostle, his reputation as a persecutor of the church preceded him. We tend to think of him as the *uber apostle* today who championed the emerging Christian church. That is undoubtedly who he ended up becoming, but it's easy to forget that he didn't start out that way. It took Paul many years to prove himself to believers.

Verse 24 is notable: "They praised God because of me." In apologetics, when we think of defending the truth of Christianity, we tend to assume we need to present lots of Scripture and robust logical arguments. Those things are certainly important, especially in formal discussions. But at the end of the day, there is no more compelling argument for the truth of Jesus than a changed life. And in all of Scripture, there is perhaps no better example of a changed life than Saul the persecutor becoming Paul the apostle. The churches in Judea heard the report of a man who used to persecute Christians but was now preaching the gospel. And when they met Paul and saw that it was true, they praised God.

Galatians 1
Discussion Questions

1. What exactly is the gospel of Jesus? What ideas must it include? What are some examples of Christian ideas that are important, but not part of the gospel?

2. How would you say the Christian church is doing when it comes to focusing on the one true gospel? How about your specific church or small group? Are there any areas where you may have begun wandering off course or mixing in other ideas?

3. The greatest danger in leading God's people astray comes from within the church (e.g., the golden calf fiasco). What do you see as the most significant internal dangers to the church today? Have you ever had to choose between pleasing God and pleasing people? How did you handle that situation?

PAUL AND THE APOSTLES

Galatians 2:1–14

❧

Modern translators inserted a new chapter at this point, but Paul is simply continuing his story. You have to wonder if the Galatians listening to this letter were aware of these events in his past. Whether this is new news or a reminder, it's clear that the apostle is selectively choosing to recount incidents that speak directly to the situation at hand. He now fast-forwards to another encounter in Jerusalem:

> ¹Then after fourteen years, I went up again to Jerusalem, this time with Barnabas. I took Titus along also. ²I went in response to a revelation and, meeting privately with those esteemed as leaders, I presented to them the gospel that I preach among the Gentiles. I wanted to be sure I was not running and had not been running my race in vain.

Paul continues to bolster his defense against the false accusations of the Judaizers, who were trying to undermine his authority by highlighting his lack of connection with the Jerusalem church. They may even have claimed that the only reason he had gone up to Jerusalem after fourteen years was because he had been summoned by the apostles to explain his heretical teachings on the law. Paul corrects the record, revealing that God Himself had directed him to visit Jerusalem: "I went in response to a revelation" (2:2).

So, Paul headed up to Jerusalem with Barnabas and Titus in tow.[1] He then makes a curious comment: "I wanted to be sure I was not running and had not been running my race in vain" (2:2). He wouldn't have been concerned about the accuracy of the gospel he was preaching. Paul already revealed that he had received this gospel from Jesus Himself and had been endorsed by Peter and James fourteen years earlier in Jerusalem. What was his concern about operating his ministry in vain?

A consistent theme in Paul's writings is unity in the body of Christ. He learned the importance of unity from Jesus, who taught, "By this everyone will know that you are my disciples, if you love one another" (John 13:35). And in His high priestly prayer, Jesus three times expresses His desire that His disciples "may be one" (John 17:11, 21, 22) even as He and God are one. Paul wanted to make sure everyone was on the same page. And because of his boldness and confidence in Christ, I don't believe he went up to Jerusalem to run his gospel by the apostles and make sure he had it right. Rather, Paul was testing the apostles to make sure *they* had it right.

Paul was not yet well-acquainted with the Jerusalem church; he didn't seem to know who was in charge. He met "with those esteemed as leaders" (2:2). Other translations say "those who seemed influential" (ESV) or "those recognized as leaders" (CSB). Paul went up to Jerusalem hoping to find the church leaders in alignment with him on the issue of the gospel for the Gentiles. Unity was his goal. If the other apostles had sided with the Judaizers and taught that Gentile believers were required to be circumcised and keep the law, Paul would have felt he was running his race in vain.

> ³Yet not even Titus, who was with me, was compelled to be circumcised, even though he was a Greek. ⁴This matter arose because some false believers had infiltrated our ranks to spy on the freedom we have in Christ Jesus and to make us slaves. ⁵We did not give in to them for a moment, so that the truth of the gospel might be preserved for you.

Paul recounts this incident because the "false believers" in Jerusalem (2:4) taught the same thing the Judaizers were teaching in Galatia. They were likely part of the same circumcision party. Paul brought Titus, an uncircumcised Gentile, with him to Jerusalem to make sure he had not been running his race in vain. He was testing the church leaders: Would they allow Titus into the family of God without requiring him to be circumcised? Indeed, they did.

To add credibility to his story, Paul specifically mentions that Barnabas was at this meeting (2:1). The Galatians knew Barnabas; he had traveled with Paul when they first shared the gospel in that area (Acts 13–14). And he witnessed the apostles' approval of Paul's gospel message in Jerusalem. Paul's message to the Galatian readers was loud and clear: even the apostles in Jerusalem agreed that circumcision is not a requirement for following Jesus. *If you don't believe me, ask Barnabas. He'll tell you it's true!*

Notice the way Paul builds his *apologia*. He is not simply claiming that the Judaizers are wrong but instead is methodically building a case based on evidence and appealing to logic, reason, and facts. So far, Paul has shared what happened, who he spoke with, where he went, and what was decided. He has produced eyewitnesses and provided not only personal testimony but the testimony of the apostles in Jerusalem, whom both the Judaizers and the Galatians accepted as authoritative.

The believers in Galatia had been argued into the Judaizers' false gospel, so Paul is taking the time to argue them out of it. This approach is not only valuable in convincing them of who is right, but *why*. After all, Jesus said the greatest commandment is "Love the Lord your God with all your heart and with all your soul and with all your *mind*" (Matt. 22:37). Apologetics is one way of living out the intellectual side of that command. It is using our minds to contend for the truth of the gospel. And Paul's incredible apologetic case against the false gospel of the Judaizers is just getting started.

In verse 4, Paul speaks of "false believers"—literally, "false brothers" (*pseudadelphous*)—who were preaching circumcision in Jerusalem during that visit. There was deception afoot; Paul says these people "had infiltrated our ranks" (2:4). This is the "danger from within" that Paul is so keenly aware of and eager to warn his readers about. And his description of the Judaizers as "false believers" provides us with another clue. Not only are they teaching a "different gospel" (1:6), but Paul questions the authenticity of their faith.

In fact, Paul says the reason these false brothers had infiltrated the ranks of the Jerusalem church was "to spy on the freedom we have in Christ Jesus and to make us slaves" (2:4). Behind the phrase "make us slaves," we find Paul's second use of the Greek root word *doulos*, "slave." He said in Galatians 1:10 that he was a *doulos* of Christ; Jesus was Paul's master. Here, he implies (and will later develop) the idea that the Judaizers see the law as their master. They want to enslave Christians to the law.

Paul's description may contain a degree of hyperbole, but his point is plain. The false teachers in Jerusalem were up to no good, and they knew it. Their intentions were contrary to the truth of the gospel. The apostle draws a clear parallel. Just as the false teachers in Jerusalem were dangerous, so, too, are the Judaizers who had slipped into the churches in Galatia to "pervert the gospel of Christ" (1:7). And just as Paul and the Jerusalem apostles "did not give in to them for a moment, so that the truth of the gospel might be preserved for you" (2:5), so, too, should the believers in Galatia reject their false teachings. This is not a secondary issue. The gospel is at stake.

The Judaizers, of course, didn't see it that way. They would not have viewed themselves as endangering anyone's freedom or trying to make anyone a slave. The circumcision party was comprised of Jewish Pharisees whose stated intention was to honor God in all they did. They wanted to bring Gentile believers into what they saw as proper alignment with the old covenant law. It seemed natural to them that all followers of the Jewish Messiah should be required to keep the same laws that God had given Israel at Sinai. These were, after all, the same laws that the psalmist taught them to delight in:

> Oh, how I love your law!
>   I meditate on it all day long.
> Your commands are always with me
>   and make me wiser than my enemies.
> I have more insight than all my teachers,
>   for I meditate on your statutes.
> I have more understanding than the elders,
>   for I obey your precepts. (Ps. 119:97–100)

The kernel of error from which the misguided motivation of the Judaizers grew can be found in many cults and false teachings. It is also the source of the "works-righteousness" theology held (directly or indirectly) by some mainstream Christians. It seems counterintuitive, but, sometimes, the thing that causes us to miss out on God is a hyperfocus on the *things* of God. (He has had to teach me this lesson more than once!) It is possible to learn about God and to serve Him without actually knowing Him. Moreover, there is a difference between doing things *for* God and doing things *with* Him. We can sometimes get so caught up in our small groups, Bible studies, kids' programs, volunteer work, and even evangelism that we fail to spend time with our Creator. This is the difference between religion and relationship.

Jesus told the Samaritan woman at the well that true worship was being loosed from its old covenant geographic moorings in Jerusalem:

> A time is coming when you will worship the Father neither on this mountain nor in Jerusalem . . . A time is coming and has now come when the true worshipers will worship the Father in the Spirit and in truth, for they are the kind of worshipers the Father seeks. God is spirit, and his worshipers must worship in the Spirit and in truth. (John 4:21, 23–24)

This has always been God's desire. He created us to live in an active relationship with Him, but we rejected His idyllic plan in the garden of Eden. When Adam disobeyed, sin entered the world. Consequently, Adam and Eve were banished from God's presence. Thanks to our merciful Father, the human story did not end there. In His enduring grace and love, God responded to our first sin by enacting a plan to redeem us and restore our access to Him.

After rescuing the people of Israel from slavery in Egypt, Yahweh made a covenant with them at Mount Sinai. He gave Israel the law which served as the terms of that covenant. As Paul will explain in Galatians 3, the law was a tutor given to guard and instruct Israel in seeking the heart of God. But even that law was not His ultimate end; God has always desired our hearts more than our ritual obedience. The psalmist writes:

> You do not delight in sacrifice, or I would bring it;
>   you do not take pleasure in burnt offerings.
> My sacrifice, O God, is a broken spirit;
>   a broken and contrite heart
>   you, God, will not despise. (Ps. 51:16–17)

Paul saw what the Judaizers had yet to realize: the law of Moses was always intended as a temporary measure. He will teach in the next chapter, "The law was our guardian until Christ came that we might be justified by faith. Now that this faith has come, we are no longer under a guardian" (3:24–25). Now that faith in Jesus has arrived, we are no longer under the old covenant law.

Because the Judaizers missed the provisional nature of the Mosaic law, they saw rituals like circumcision as an ongoing expression of obedience to Yahweh. This perspective was part of the theological debris that still littered the land after the "Jesus explosion." Paul understood the changes Christ had introduced with His new covenant. He understood, for example, that circumcision was given under the old covenant to distinguish the nation of Israel from the other nations. Under Jesus, however, there was no further need for that ritual. While an ethnic distinction remains, Jewish and Gentile believers are "one in Christ Jesus" (3:28).

What the Judaizers saw as an enduring expression of obedience, Paul, a proud Jew from birth, had come to view as a form of slavery as compared to our freedom in Christ. He declared that the circumcision party wanted "to make us slaves" (2:4), adding, "We did not give in to them for a moment, so that the truth of the gospel might be preserved for you" (2:5). For Paul, circumcision was a gospel issue. Describing it as slavery would have been offensive to the Judaizers. However, we'll see Paul double and triple down on the theme of "slavery versus freedom" throughout this epistle.

A Closer Look at Slavery in Galatians

The ears of Americans living in a post-Civil War era are especially attuned to the word *slavery*. It is a shameful reminder of an ugly institution that marred our nation's past and resonates to this day. For Paul and his audience, the concept of slavery had a similar national connotation, though in a much different setting. For first-century Jews, the word *slavery* not only evoked images of Egypt, where their ancestors spent centuries in chains and forced labor but also the miraculous, nation-defining exodus in which "The LORD brought us out of Egypt with a mighty hand and an outstretched arm, with great terror and with signs and wonders" (Deut. 26:8).

The Israelites' escape from Egypt brought them directly to the foot of Mount Sinai, where the Lord made a covenant with them and gave them His law. As a formally trained Jewish man, Paul was well aware that the law is God-ordained and just. He elsewhere calls it "holy, righteous and good" (Rom. 7:12). And the law is undoubtedly included in his statement to Timothy:

> All Scripture is God-breathed and is useful for teaching, rebuking, correcting and training in righteousness, so that the servant of God may be thoroughly equipped for every good work. (2 Tim. 3:16–17)

Yet, in his letter to the Galatians, Paul continually compares the law to slavery. What's going on? In this epistle, Paul draws a stark contrast between slavery and freedom to make a particular point about the law. This is especially evident in chapter 4 when he contrasts slaves and heirs and presents an allegory of a slave woman and a free woman. This concept didn't originate with Paul; it comes directly from Jesus. Consider the conversation recorded in John's gospel:

To the Jews who had believed him, Jesus said, "If you hold to my teaching, you are really my disciples. Then you will know the truth, and the truth will set you free."

They answered him, "We are Abraham's descendants and have never been slaves of anyone. How can you say that we shall be set free?"

Jesus replied, "Very truly I tell you, everyone who sins is a slave to sin. Now a slave has no permanent place in the family, but a son belongs to it forever. So if the Son sets you free, you will be free indeed. (John 8:31-36)

Every concept Jesus speaks of in this passage is picked up and developed by Paul in Galatians: freedom in Christ, slavery, sin, Abraham's offspring, and a place in God's family.

Jesus says, "Everyone who sins is a slave to sin" (John 8:34). Paul says the law "imprisoned everything under sin" (3:22 ESV). We all know that sin is fun and even intoxicating at first. It promises us the freedom to do whatever we want whenever we want. *What happens in Vegas stays in Vegas.* No boundaries, baby! But one way or another, we all inevitably come to realize that, like the serpent in the garden, sin is whispering lies in our ears. It is, in reality, a cruel slave master that ultimately dominates our lives. Sin subdues, controls, restrains, and ultimately kills us.

Paul's point in Galatians is that the law keeps us chained to our sin and there is no way to escape it on our own. It reveals our sin but offers no ultimate solution for sin. This is the aspect of the law Paul is thinking of when he compares it to slavery. He shakes his head and asks the Galatians, "Tell me, you who want to be under the law, are you not aware of what the law says?" (4:21). To seek justification before God through the law is a fool's errand. No human being has ever been able to do so. The people of Israel tried and failed so miserably that they broke the covenant that came with the law (Jer. 31:31–34). The bar was just too high.

To fail at the law is to inherit its curses: "All who rely on the works of the law are under a curse" (3:10). Therefore, God, in His mercy, sent His Son to free us in a most unexpected way: "Christ redeemed us from the curse of the law by becoming a curse for us" (3:13). This is why Paul can say, "The law was our guardian until Christ came that we might be justified by faith" (3:24). The law points us to Christ, who came to set us free. And as Jesus said, "If the Son sets you free, you will be free indeed" (John 8:36). Paul echoes: "It is for freedom that Christ has set us free. Stand firm, then, and do not let yourselves be burdened again by a yoke of slavery" (5:1).

It's easy to look back on the beliefs of the first-century Judaizers as antiquated and outdated. Yet there are still Judaizers among us today. Those same false beliefs live on in the theology broadly known as *Torahism*, which is practiced by groups such as the Hebrew Roots Movement, Torah Keepers, and various other flavors of "Torah-observant" Christianity. Like the Judaizers, these modern groups teach that Christians are required to keep all of the rituals prescribed in the old covenant law and that not doing so is sinful and disobedient.

However, there is a critical difference between the Judaizers of

Paul's day and modern-day "Torah keepers." First-century Judaizers were Jews raised in the Jewish faith who were trying to find their way during the first days of the new covenant without the help of a NT. While dangerous, their confusion on these issues is at least understandable. Conversely, "Torah-observant" Christians today are Gentiles raised in the Christian faith who were never under the law of Moses and have always had a NT. There is no good excuse for their confusion.

More broadly, the spirit of the first-century Judaizers lives on today in overly legalistic factions of Christendom. Some Bible teachers and churches leave little room for grace on certain issues. As we'll see in this letter to the Galatians, Paul preaches a mature, biblical balance between liberty and justice. On one side of the road, he warns against the ditch of legalism, which elevates rules and rituals over the heart of God. As Geerhardus Vos famously wrote, "Legalism lacks the supreme sense of worship. It obeys but it does not adore."[2] Some of Jesus's harshest criticisms were leveled against the sin of legalism.

Opposite legalism lies the danger of *antinomianism* or lawlessness. This is the rebellious rejection of any limit on our thoughts or behaviors. We see this thinking in the "carnal Christianity" (or "free grace") movement of the late twentieth century. This theology says that as long as we profess faith in Jesus, we're saved, even if our lives show no evidence of a changed heart. More recently, antinomianism can be found running rampant in progressive Christianity. This is a movement admirably centered on Jesus's core teaching to "love one another" (John 13:34–35).[3] However, progressive Christianity ultimately abandons the biblical definition of love and God's timeless standards of morality in favor of modern virtues such as inclusion, sexual expression, and political activism.

Modern Christians admittedly face a difficult new frontier in which we must live out our faith. Finding our footing on the ever-shifting sands of a postmodern, post-Christian culture can be challenging. At the forefront of this issue is society's evolving views on sexuality. The boundaries God placed around healthy and proper sexual expression—limited to one man and one woman in the context of marriage—were given for our good and for the flourishing of the human race. Surely God knows best. Yet these boundaries are roundly seen as antiquated today, even among many Christians.

It is increasingly difficult to honor God with our bodies in a hypersexualized culture. On top of that, most Christians (me included) know and love someone who falls somewhere on the spectrum of LGBT+. How do we continually show the love of Christ without compromising our loyalty to His Word? Our only hope in navigating such treacherous waters is to daily cling to the guidance of the Holy Spirit.

When we deal with the issue of sexual sin, it's important to remember what Jesus said to the Pharisees when they brought Him a woman caught in adultery: "Let any one of you who is without sin be the first to throw a stone at her" (John 8:7).[4] However, the story doesn't end there:

> Those who heard began to go away one at a time, the older ones first, until only Jesus was left, with the woman still standing there. Jesus straightened up and asked her, "Woman, where are they? Has no one condemned you?"
>
> "No one, sir," she said.
>
> "Then neither do I condemn you," Jesus declared. "Go now and leave your life of sin." (John 8:9–11)

Jesus showed this woman mercy rather than condemnation. But He did not minimize the sinfulness of her actions or suggest it was okay for her to continue in them. Rather, He modeled for us a perfect balance of grace and truth.

Believers today are called to "act justly and to love mercy and to walk humbly with your God" (Mic. 6:8). The mature Christian remains aware of the pitfalls on both sides of the road: legalism on the right and lawlessness on the left. Interestingly, as Sinclair Ferguson notes, both extremes essentially commit the same error. They view God's law as separate from His person and character.

> Antinomianism and legalism are not so much antithetical to each other as they are both antithetical to grace. This is why Scripture never prescribes one as the antidote for the other. Rather grace, God's grace in Christ in our union with Christ, is the antidote to both.[5]

After describing how he and the apostles in Jerusalem rejected the idea that Titus, or any other believer, should be circumcised (2:1–5), Paul continues his story:

> [6]As for those who were held in high esteem—whatever they were makes no difference to me; God does not show favoritism—they added nothing to my message. [7]On the contrary, they recognized that I had been entrusted with the task of preaching the gospel to the uncircumcised, just as Peter had been to the circumcised. [8]For God, who was at work in Peter as an apostle to the circumcised, was also at work in me as an apostle to the Gentiles. [9]James, Cephas and John, those esteemed as pillars, gave me and Barnabas the right hand of fellowship when they recognized the grace given to me. They agreed that we should go to the Gentiles, and they to the circumcised. [10]All they asked was that we should continue to remember the poor, the very thing I had been eager to do all along.

The church leadership in Jerusalem did not challenge or change Paul's message. They were all in agreement. In fact, they acknowledged Paul as an apostle to the Gentiles (the uncircumcised) in the same way that Peter was an apostle to the Jews (the circumcised). They even gave him "the right hand of fellowship" (2:9), recognizing their partnership as ministers of the gospel. Paul systematically disproves the idea that he is a lone wolf preaching an aberrant message. On the contrary, he received the full backing of the "pillars" (2:9) of Jerusalem.

The theological impact of the Jerusalem meeting was far-reaching. It was an unexpected blow for the Judaizers. Under the old covenant law, circumcision was commanded by God Himself (Lev. 12:3). Under the new covenant, it was no longer required. And Paul's argument to the Galatians isn't simply "because I said so." Peter, James, and the other leaders in Jerusalem also agreed that Gentiles do not need to be circumcised in order to join God's family. The Jerusalem Council would uphold that same conclusion just a few years later (Acts 15:1–29).

The expiration of ritual circumcision as an obligation took decades to sink in with many Jewish believers. But not all. The apostles who walked and ministered alongside Jesus accepted this change more quickly. If they had believed that the law of Moses was binding on all Christians, they would have required Titus to be circumcised. But they didn't. This will be a major line of argument for Paul in the coming chapters as he shifts from historical evidence to theological arguments.

PAUL OPPOSES PETER

Galatians 2:11–14

After recounting the historic meeting in Jerusalem, Paul hits the fast-forward button again, and the setting changes to Antioch:

> ¹¹When Cephas came to Antioch, I opposed him to his face, because he stood condemned. ¹²For before certain men came from James, he used to eat with the Gentiles. But when they arrived, he began to draw back and separate himself from the Gentiles because he was afraid of those who belonged to the circumcision group. ¹³The other Jews joined him in his hypocrisy, so that by their hypocrisy even Barnabas was led astray. ¹⁴When I saw that they were not acting in line with the truth of the gospel, I said to Cephas in front of them all, "You are a Jew, yet you live like a Gentile and not like a Jew. How is it, then, that you force Gentiles to follow Jewish customs?"

This passage is bursting with theological implications. It reveals a significant event in the early church and says much about the relationship between Christians and the law of Moses. Sometime between the "right hand of fellowship" in Jerusalem (2:9) and this confrontation in Antioch, Peter went from eating with the Gentiles to separating from them.

Paul writes, "For before certain men came from James, he used to eat with the Gentiles" (2:12). It was public knowledge that Peter had been sharing a table of fellowship with Gentle believers. He had, after all, been the first apostle chosen by God to preach to Gentiles, as we learn from his story about leading the first Gentiles to faith in Jesus (Acts 10:24–48). And then "certain men came from James" (2:12). Paul leaves these men unnamed, indicating only that they came from among James's flock, the Jerusalem church. When they arrived in Antioch, Peter "began to draw back and separate himself from the Gentiles because he was afraid of those who belonged to the circumcision group" (2:12). These Judaizers may have been the same men James would later speak of at the Jerusalem Council: "We have heard that some went out from us without our authorization and disturbed you, troubling your minds by what they said" (Acts 15:24). But how could they convince a believer like the Peter to lose step with the gospel (2:14)?

In first-century Hebrew culture, eating with others meant accepting them as social equals. This is one of the reasons the Pharisees were offended by Jesus eating with sinners and tax collectors.[1] More significantly, sharing a table with Gentiles was a big deal because of the Torah's dietary restrictions. The old covenant food laws did not function merely as a religious observance. "They also acted as a practical, day-to-day social barrier to other cultures. The food laws made it difficult for the Israelites to interact with the Gentiles around them because of the risk of ritual defilement through the unclean foods served."[2]

Paul describes a time when Peter enjoyed table fellowship with all believers, Jews and Gentiles alike. They were one family in Christ. In doing so, Peter not only acknowledged that they were of equal value in God's kingdom but also telegraphed to the church that the old covenant food laws were no longer in effect. However, under pressure from the Judaizers, he wavered. Peter, raised as an orthodox Jew, seems to struggle to understand this message. In fact, let's take a brief look at Peter's track record with the kosher food laws. It will shed valuable light on the conflict in Antioch between Paul and Peter.

A Closer Look at Peter and Kosher Food

There is a pattern in Scripture of Peter struggling to understand the change in the food laws. Jesus told the Pharisees:

> What goes into someone's mouth does not defile them, but what comes out of their mouth, that is what defiles them. . . . Don't you see that whatever enters the mouth goes into the stomach and then out of the body? But the things that come out of a person's mouth come from the heart, and these defile them. (Matt. 15:11, 17–18)

We are not made ritually unclean by the food we consume but by the evil thoughts we harbor in our hearts, which are revealed to the world through our words.

> Then the disciples came to him and asked, "Do you know that the Pharisees were offended when they heard this?" (Matt. 15:12)

The old covenant law taught that what goes into the body *can* defile a person and make him or her ritually unclean. Leviticus 11 contains a detailed list of animals that God declared unclean and says that eating any of these prohibited creatures defiles a person (Lev. 11:43). Yet in Matthew 15,[3] Jesus teaches that we are not defiled by what goes into our mouths but rather by our evil thoughts. The Pharisees were offended and Jesus's disciples were confused. Guess which disciple spoke up and asked Jesus to explain Himself.

Peter said, "Explain the parable to us." (Matt. 15:15)

The disciples were having trouble wrapping their minds around what Jesus said. From our modern perspective, it seems pretty simple. It is not the food we eat but the wicked things we hold in our hearts that defile us, like lust, greed, and hatred. In the context of first-century Judaism, however, this idea was so astonishing that it felt wrong. The Mosaic food laws were so baked into (pun intended) the rhythm of Hebrew life that even the Lord's disciples had trouble working out what He was saying.

Indeed, Jesus's lesson did not seem to land with Peter. Later, just before the apostle would first preach the gospel to the Gentiles, God had to remind Peter about it again. In Acts 10, Peter fell into a trance and had a vision:

He saw heaven opened and something like a large sheet being let down to earth by its four corners. It contained all kinds of four-footed animals, as well as reptiles and birds. Then a voice told him, "Get up, Peter. Kill and eat."

"Surely not, Lord!" Peter replied. "I have never eaten anything impure or unclean." (Acts 10:11-14)

Peter was so committed to Jewish tradition and so devoted to the law of Moses that he would openly oppose a command from Jesus Himself. The Lord directed Peter to eat, and the apostle ironically responded, "Surely not, Lord!" (Acts 10:14). To address someone as *kyrios* (Lord) is to acknowledge their authority over you. Yet Peter uses this title for Jesus while *challenging* His authority. So, Jesus rebukes Peter: "What God has made clean, do not call common" (Acts 10:15 ESV). This exchange happened three times (Acts 10:16); Peter is a little hardheaded! The Lord then sent him to the house of a Gentile named Cornelius, where the apostle announced:

You are well aware that it is against our law for a Jew to associate with or visit a Gentile. But God has shown me that I should not call anyone impure or unclean. (Acts 10:28)

Why would Peter say that God showed him not to call any *person* impure or unclean? His rooftop vision spoke only of animals. Without being explicitly told, Peter knew that the command Jesus had repeated three times— "What God has made clean, do not call common"—also referred to people. As a good Torah-observant Jew, Peter was aware that unclean food and unclean people are connected in the Torah.

In Leviticus, God told Israel:

You must therefore make a distinction between clean and unclean animals and between unclean and clean birds. Do not defile yourselves by any animal or bird or anything that moves along the ground—those that I have set apart as unclean for you. You are to be holy to me because I, the Lord, am holy, and I have set you apart from the nations to be my own. (Lev. 20:25–26)

Israel was to be *qadosh* (holy), which means "set apart for God." *Qadosh* carries the idea of distinction and uniqueness, something removed from common use. When God made His covenant with Israel, He declared, "Although the whole earth is mine, you will be for me a kingdom of priests and a *holy* nation" (Exod. 19:5–6, emphasis added). He also said, "I have set *you apart* from the nations to be my own" (Lev. 20:26, emphasis added). Israel was to "make a distinction between clean and unclean animals" (Lev. 20:25) as a continual, daily reminder that God had made a distinction between ancient Israel and the rest of the nations.

Under the Sinai covenant, the people of Israel were set apart through a number of commands unique to them. Israel alone was required to rest on the seventh day of the week, keep God's calendar of Torah feasts, be circumcised on the eighth day, and avoid eating specific animals. None of these commandments applied to other nations. They were not expected of Egyptians, Hittites, Babylonians, Assyrians, or any other people. These were outward markers that told the world that Israel belonged to Yahweh.

The *set-apartness* of Israel is the reason behind the seemingly arbitrary list of prohibited animals in Leviticus 11. The text provides a partial basis on which animals were to be determined clean or unclean.[4] But why *that* basis? The Bible doesn't say. But when you think about it, this makes more sense than if the animals were forbidden for obvious reasons. For example, if certain animals were prohibited because they carried parasites and caused sickness, Gentiles would avoid those same animals and Israel would cease to be distinct. Leviticus 11 would become a list of animals everyone avoided eating because they caused health problems. Rather, Israel was special and *qadosh* because it observed this prohibited list for no other reason than Yahweh commanded it.

These dietary regulations had a significant social impact. Much like today, the sharing of meals played a central role in ancient Near Eastern culture. Food and drink were at the hub of social interactions, business transactions, and even diplomatic relations between nations. Israel's unique diet made it challenging for them to interact with Gentiles on a regular basis if they wanted to maintain covenant faithfulness.

It was this link between food and people that led to Peter's conclusion about the vision in Acts 10. When God reminded him that He had made all food clean, Peter realized there was no reason to object to visiting the house of the Gentile Cornelius. Under the old covenant, God used food as one way to set Israel apart from the Gentile nations. Under the new covenant, God used a vision of food to show Peter that Jews were no longer to be set apart from Gentiles. The gospel is for all nations!

Peter knew God had opened His door to all people. He was there when Jesus taught about what truly defiles a person.[5] But he had apparently fallen back into his old Jewish way of thinking because he had to be reminded of it in Acts 10. And his story didn't end there. Peter had evidently fallen back into that thinking a third time, which caused Paul to call him to the carpet on this very same issue in Galatians 2.[6]

Notice the progression with Peter. "For before certain men came from James, he used to eat with the Gentiles" (2:12). After Peter visited Cornelius, he had been eating with Gentiles. "But when they arrived, he began to draw back and separate himself from the Gentiles because he was afraid of those who belonged to the circumcision group" (2:12). Isn't that interesting? Peter was afraid of the Judaizers, and his fear caused him to waver. This is reminiscent of his attempt to walk on the water:

> "Lord, if it's you," Peter replied, "tell me to come to you on the water."
>
> "Come," he said.
>
> Then Peter got down out of the boat, walked on the water and came toward Jesus. But when he saw the wind, he was afraid and, beginning to sink, cried out, "Lord, save me!"
>
> Immediately Jesus reached out his hand and caught him. "You of little faith," he said, "why did you doubt?" (Matt. 14:28–31)

A similar episode is unfolding in Antioch. Under pressure from the Judaizers, Peter, of little faith, began to question whether he should eat with Gentiles. He wavered, and Paul called him on it. Peter was arguably the most well-known apostle at the time. His equivocation on this issue was leading others astray as well: "The other Jews joined him in his hypocrisy, so that by their hypocrisy even Barnabas was led astray" (2:13). Peter's uncertainty had caused an avalanche of duplicity among early Jewish believers. Because his transgressions were committed publicly and had led others in the church astray, Paul felt justified in publicly reprimanding Peter:

> When I saw that they were not acting in line with the truth of the gospel, I said to Cephas in front of them all, "You are a Jew, yet you live like a Gentile and not like a Jew. How is it, then, that you force Gentiles to follow Jewish customs?" (2:14)

There are two big takeaways from this passage. First, Paul reiterates that this is a gospel matter. Peter and the other Jews in Antioch were deviating from the truth of the gospel, just like the Judaizers in Galatia. Second, this passage speaks to Paul's apostolic credentials and authority. Here is the newest apostle, publicly rebuking the oldest and most well-known apostle.[7] He is worked up about this situation!

Peter may not have realized that his withdrawing from fellowship with Gentile Christians was signaling that they weren't as good or worthy as Jewish believers. It was a public snub that cast them as second-class citizens who, in some sense, lacked the fullness of the gospel. Otherwise, why separate from them? Commentator Andrew Knowles captures this danger well:

> If Peter's hypocrisy had infected the whole church, the result would have been a split between Jewish and Gentile Christians. It may even have caused the true gospel to be lost—sunk without trace beneath the waves of Jewish legalism.[8]

In his rebuke, Paul makes a somewhat knotty statement. He tells Peter, "You are a Jew, yet you live like a Gentile and not like a Jew. How is it, then, that you force Gentiles to follow Jewish customs?" (2:14). Peter, an orthodox Jew, had lived among the Gentiles for a time, sharing meals with them. He was unconcerned about what they ate and had effectively torn down the social barrier between Jews and Gentiles in the body of Christ. And Paul wants to know how Peter can then turn around and "force Gentiles to follow Jewish customs" (2:14). Peter wasn't merely separating from the Gentile believers; he had joined the Judaizers in pressuring them to observe the Jewish food laws in order to be accepted into fellowship. This is precisely what the false teachers in Galatia promoted.

If Peter responded to Paul's reprimand, it's not recorded here. Paul simply says, "He stood condemned" (2:11). Peter acted contrary to his convictions and betrayed the truth that the Gentiles are now accepted into God's family without keeping the old covenant law. By bending his knee to the Judaizers, Peter was shaming his brothers and sisters in Christ and "not acting in line with the truth of the gospel" (2:14). Paul's account is a warning to the believers in Galatia who might be tempted to do what Peter did. It also applies to Christians today who are dividing the body of Christ over secondary issues and social customs. Who are we to require something of our brothers and sisters that God does not?

JUSTIFIED
BY FAITH
Galatians 2:15–21

⤳

Paul now pivots away from his rebuke of Peter to address a broader audience:

> [15]We who are Jews by birth and not sinful Gentiles [16]know that a person is not justified by the works of the law, but by faith in Jesus Christ. So we, too, have put our faith in Christ Jesus that we may be justified by faith in Christ and not by the works of the law, because by the works of the law no one will be justified.

Paul addresses Jewish believers and Judaizers alike. He uses a phrase common in first-century Jewish circles: "sinful Gentiles" (2:15). At that time, many religious Jews adopted the view that "We have the law; everyone else is a sinner." In fact, it was commonplace for the word *Gentile* to be followed by the word *sinner* in daily conversation. Paul declares that even "we who are Jews by birth" (2:15)—those to whom the law was given and who were brought up to keep that law—know that no one is counted righteous in God's eyes through works of the law.

Notice the brilliant way the apostle structured this statement. Biblical Greek does not have punctuation; there are no exclamation points, italics, or underscores. Therefore, repetition is the primary method for drawing a reader's attention to an important point. And Paul manages to repeat himself three times in a single verse (see bold type):

> A person is **not justified by the works of the law**, but by faith in Jesus Christ. So we, too, have put our faith in Christ Jesus that we may be justified by faith in Christ and **not by the works of the law**, because **by the works of the law no one will be justified**. (2:16)

Paul does not want his readers to miss this point. In a statement aimed squarely at the false teachings of the Judaizers, he stresses that keeping the law of Moses justifies no one.

This is the first appearance of *justification* in Galatians. It might even be—if you believe as I do that Galatians is Paul's earliest epistle—the first appearance of that word in all of Paul's writings. The biblical concept of justification plays a significant role in the apostle's argument and explains why he takes such a heated tone. The stakes are incredibly high. In fact, this is the very issue that shook the church in the sixteenth century and led to the Reformation. Martin Luther considered justification the doctrine on which the church would ultimately stand or fall.

Paul's pithy statements about justification in Galatians are later filled out in much greater detail in Romans. So, let's take a moment to explore this issue before we continue on. It will help us understand Paul's heated confrontation with Peter in Antioch and the remarkable case he will make in chapters 3–4.

A Closer Look at Justification

Justification (Greek: *dikaioō*) is an idea borrowed from the legal world that refers to the decisions of courts and judges. Therefore, theologians refer to justification as a *forensic* term. It has to do with justice; it's how God responds to our faith in Jesus and what He does with the guilt of our sins. If He were to "wink" at sin and evil and let it all go unpunished, He wouldn't be a fair, just, and righteous God. So, as Paul will explain in Galatians 3, Jesus stepped in and took upon Himself the punishment necessary to fulfill God's requirement for ultimate justice once and for all. How does that work?

There is a short passage in Romans 3 that reads as if someone had asked Paul to explain what he meant in Galatians 2:15–16. It begins:

> But now apart from the law the righteousness of God has been made known, to which the Law and the Prophets testify. This righteousness is given through faith in Jesus Christ to all who believe. (Rom. 3:21–22)

This is the biblical definition of justification: "Righteousness given through faith in Jesus." Notice how deeply connected justification and salvation are. In fact, while theologians like to maintain a technical distinction between the two—seeing justification as a fundamental component of salvation—from the believer's perspective they are essentially the same thing. Both flow from the same faith in Christ, and neither can exist without the other. We cannot be saved without being declared righteous by God (justified), and we cannot be declared righteous by God without also inheriting salvation. This is an important concept to understand. Trying to have one without the other would be like trying to score the most points in the Super Bowl without winning the game. It's just not possible.

Romans 3:22 says justification (and therefore salvation) has been revealed "apart from the law." Paul says the same thing in Galatians: "A person is not justified by the works of the law, but by faith in Jesus Christ" (2:16). The passage in Romans 3 continues:

> There is no difference between Jew and Gentile, for all have sinned and fall short of the glory of God, and all are justified freely by his grace through the redemption that came by Christ Jesus. (Rom. 3:22-24)

No one can achieve perfect righteousness on his or her own. We all fall short. That includes both "Jews by birth" and "sinful Gentiles" (2:15). However—and here is the good news of the gospel—by the grace of God we are all given the opportunity to be declared righteous by placing our faith in Jesus. In fact, we are "justified freely." Other translations (such as the ESV) say, "as a gift." And, of course, if you have to work for a gift, it's not a gift; it's a wage![1] The only work required for justification is the work of Jesus. And faith in Him is the only requirement for being declared righteous in God's eyes.

Paul continues in Romans:

> God presented Christ as a sacrifice of atonement,
> through the shedding of his blood—to be received
> by faith. (Rom. 3:25)

This language was intentionally used to bring to mind the sacrifices for sin detailed in the Torah. The phrase "sacrifice of atonement" is just one word in Greek: *hilastērion*. This term carries extraordinary OT imagery often missed in English translations. It is a profound foreshadowing of the work of Christ.

Under OT law, the *ark of the covenant* (a wooden chest covered in pure gold and topped with an elaborate lid) was placed in the innermost room of the temple called the *Most Holy Place*. Only one person in all of Israel was allowed to enter this room, and just once a year: on *Yom Kippur*, the Day of Atonement. To atone for the sins of Israel, here is what would happen.[2]

In the outer courtyard of the temple, the high priest would sacrifice a bull and a goat at the altar. He would then take the blood into the temple, passing through the curtain into the Most Holy Place where he was in the presence of Yahweh Himself. The priest would then sprinkle the blood of the sacrifice on the elaborate lid of the ark, which was called the "atonement cover" or "mercy seat." And that atonement cover is precisely what the Greek word *hilastērion* refers to. This was how and where ancient Israel atoned for its sins under the law.

So, in Romans 3, when Paul says God "presented Christ as a sacrifice of atonement (*hilastērion*) through the shedding of his blood" (Rom. 3:25), he is linking the Torah's process for sin atonement directly to Jesus. Those ancient rituals, repeated year after year, were ultimately given to point us to Jesus, our ultimate "atonement cover," who has fulfilled the requirement for sin sacrifice once and for all. It is His blood, not the blood of bulls and goats, that brings final atonement.[3] Paul's point in Romans 3 is that this redemption did not come through the law but is "received by faith" (Rom. 3:25).

Why did God choose to do it this way? Paul offers two reasons. First:

> He did this to demonstrate his righteousness, because in his forbearance he had left the sins committed beforehand unpunished. (Rom. 3:25)

In an astounding act of mercy, God chose to leave all sin in the world up to that point unpunished. He suspended ultimate judgment until Christ arrived to take the punishment on Himself. What incredible love! The second reason is this:

> He did it to demonstrate his righteousness at the present time, so as to be just and the one who justifies those who have faith in Jesus. (Rom. 3:26)

God placed the punishment for our sins on His Son "so as to be just." Justice demands consequences for sin. And God is also "the one who justifies." He paid the price Himself. Paul explains in Philippians 2 how Jesus:

Who, being in very nature God,

did not consider equality with God something to be

used to his own advantage;

rather, he made himself nothing

by taking the very nature of a servant,

being made in human likeness.

And being found in appearance as a man,

he humbled himself

by becoming obedient to death—

even death on a cross! (Philippians 2:6–8)

And, therefore, "There is now no condemnation [charge of guilt] for those who are in Christ Jesus" (Rom. 8:1). This, my friends, is the staggering shout-it-from-the-rooftops good news of the gospel of Jesus.

Like the Judaizers in Galatia, most of us flirt with the idea that at some level our salvation needs to be earned. Surely, we need to do *something*—some small display of goodness or righteousness—to be worthy, right? That's how it works in almost every other area of our lives. Our charm and personality earn us friends. Our demonstrations of love and loyalty earn us a spouse. Our talent and knowledge earn us a job, and our continued performance ensures the paychecks keep coming. Through our behavior, we gain the acceptance of friends and colleagues alike. But that is not how God's kingdom works. Our salvation is not a wage we earn or a reward we deserve because we are good. Rather, it's a gift bestowed by God because *He* is good.

This is the very point Paul drives home in Galatians 2. It's why works-righteousness belief systems are so dangerous. Even if they don't say so explicitly—and some may even flat-out deny it—their theology is built on the implicit assumption that keeping God's commandments makes us just a little more righteous in His eyes. The first-century Judaizers displayed a flagrant form of this kind of self-righteousness. Yet it can also be found to some degree in the heart of every Christian, including me.

It is incredibly difficult for our finite human minds to fully comprehend the infinite depth of the grace of God. While doing good works and keeping God's commands are righteous activities—indeed, this is what Christians were made for (Eph. 2:10)—no amount of good deeds can add even a microgram to the perfect righteousness of Jesus credited to all who place their faith in Him. We can't make ourselves righteous enough, but God can. And, more than that, He *does*.

Romans 4 says:

> To the one who does not work but trusts God who justifies the ungodly, their faith is credited as righteousness . . . God credits righteousness apart from works. (Rom. 4:5, 6)

The righteousness God credits to us is not something we earned by doing good things or being a good person. In fact, it is not contingent on any goodness we have in us. "God . . . justifies the *ungodly*" (Rom. 4:5, emphasis added). That means sinners like you and me. When we are justified, God credits to us a righteousness that comes from outside ourselves. It is the perfect righteousness earned by Jesus.

All these concepts merge and coalesce into a single, beautiful truth. To be declared righteous by God is to be saved. Justification is the gift of salvation. "Since we have been justified through faith, we have peace with God through our Lord Jesus Christ" (Rom. 5:1). Understanding this connection is a key that unlocks the book of Galatians. When we place our faith in Jesus, we are justified (declared righteous) and reconciled to God (saved).

When Paul speaks of "justification" in Galatians, he includes the full experience of salvation. Those who are justified are saved; they are in a right relationship with God. And in Galatians 2:16 alone, Paul repeats three times that we are not justified by works of the law but by faith in Christ. This truth fueled his heated confrontation with Peter in Antioch: *How dare you try to drive a wedge between believing Jews and Gentiles based on works of the law!*

Paul continues by posing and answering a question he anticipates from his readers:

> [17]But if, in seeking to be justified in Christ, we Jews find ourselves also among the sinners, doesn't that mean that Christ promotes sin? Absolutely not! [18]If I rebuild what I destroyed, then I really would be a lawbreaker.

We saw earlier that, in first-century Jewish thinking, being without the law meant being a sinner. So, when Paul speaks of Jewish believers finding themselves "among the sinners," he is asking, *If we Jews try to seek justification before God apart from the law (like the sinful Gentiles do), doesn't that make us sinners too?* This highlights one of the most pressing theological questions in the early Christian church: How do Gentiles fit into this new Jesus movement and become followers of the Jewish Messiah? Paul's letter to the Galatians was written to bring clarity to the confusion that persisted in the aftermath of the theological "Jesus bomb." He anticipated an argument from the false teachers in Galatia: If justification by faith eliminates the law, isn't it encouraging sinful living? Legalists ask the same thing today.

I can't tell you how many times I've been confronted by a "Torah-observant" Christian[4] who challenged, "If the law of Moses is no longer in effect, is it okay to murder and commit adultery?" This is the same fallacious question posed by the Judaizers. They mistakenly conclude that if someone merely needed to believe in Jesus to be saved, he or she would be free from all moral obligations. Paul flatly rejects this idea by pointing out that if justification apart from the law meant we can freely sin, this would make Jesus a promoter of sin, which He is "Absolutely not!" (2:17). Jesus did not shed His blood on the cross as our sacrifice of atonement in order to secure our freedom to sin but rather our freedom *from* sin.

Paul next switches to the first person to drive his point home: "If I rebuild what I destroyed, then I really would be a lawbreaker" (2:18). If we try to pursue justification by keeping the law, this only reveals that we are truly lawbreakers. Alan Cole remarks:

> The Judaizers, with their reintroduction of law-keeping as an essential of salvation, are painfully rebuilding the very structure of human 'merit' that, for Paul, had come crashing in ruins on the Damascus road.[5]

Paul's first-person comment subtly targets Peter, who had withdrawn from Gentile fellowship and returned to the law, rebuilding what had previously been torn down. If a believer trusts Jesus alone for salvation (as Peter had done) and shares the gospel so that others can be saved through faith in Him (as Peter had done), but then returns to the law (as Peter had also done), it undermines the truth of the gospel.

Paul goes on to explain from personal experience why he uses such strong language:

> [19]For through the law I died to the law so that I might live for God. [20]I have been crucified with Christ and I no longer live, but Christ lives in me. The life I now live in the body, I live by faith in the Son of God, who loved me and gave himself for me. [21]I do not set aside the grace of God, for if righteousness could be gained through the law, Christ died for nothing!

When Paul came to faith in Jesus, he died to the law so that he might live for God. What an incredible statement! The death and resurrection of Jesus freed us from the law and its curses (3:13). This is why Paul describes the act of placing one's faith in Christ and then returning to the law as "rebuild[ing] what I destroyed" (2:18). Once we've received the perfect righteousness of Christ, there is no going back to our own self-powered righteousness. Doing so would only reveal how sinful we are (2:18).

Notice the profound contrast between dying and living in this passage:

> I died to the law so that I might live for God. I have been crucified with Christ and I no longer live, but Christ lives in me. The life I now live in the body, I live by faith in the Son of God. (2:19–20)

Paul is obviously not speaking of physical death. So, in what sense did he "[die] to the law" (2:19)? In what sense was he "crucified with Christ" (2:20) and therefore could say "I no longer live" (2:20)? The answer touches on what theologians call *incorporation*. This is the process through which believers are brought into a profound and intimate union with Christ. Exploring this theological theme in depth would take us well beyond the scope of this book. However, we need to touch on it briefly to get a sense of what Paul teaches in Galatians. Once again, we turn to the text of Romans to see how he develops this theme of dying to the law.

In Romans 7, Paul uses the illustration of a married woman being released from the law of marriage when her husband dies. He concludes:

> So, my brothers and sisters, you also died to the law through the body of Christ, that you might belong to another, to him who was raised from the dead, in order that we might bear fruit for God. For when we were in the realm of the flesh, the sinful passions aroused by the law were at work in us, so that we bore fruit for death. But now, by dying to what once bound us, we have been released from the law so that we serve in the new way of the Spirit, and not in the old way of the written code. (Rom. 7:4–6)

For Paul, death is a metaphor for being released. In the same way a married woman is released from the law of marriage when her husband dies, followers of Jesus are released from the old covenant law because of the death of Christ. This is precisely what Paul means when he writes, "I died to the law so that I might live for God" (2:19). Through faith in Jesus, "we have been released from the law so that we serve in the new way of the Spirit, and not in the old way of the written code" (Rom. 7:6).

What about the curious phrase "through the law I died to the law" (2:19)? Here again, Paul points his readers back to the history of the faith. God requires that His law be fulfilled. Jesus told us so in the Sermon on the Mount: "Do not think that I have come to abolish the Law or the Prophets; I have not come to abolish them but to fulfill them." (Matt. 5:17). And a couple years later, after His resurrection, Jesus appeared to the disciples and declared that they had witnessed that fulfillment:

> This is what I told you while I was still with you: Everything must be fulfilled that is written about me in the Law of Moses, the Prophets and the Psalms . . . You are witnesses of these things. (Luke 24:44–45, 48)

This is precisely what Paul is getting at: "For through the law I died to the law" (2:19). Through the law's demand to be fulfilled and man's inability to do so, Jesus came and fulfilled the law, thus releasing us from it. Paul elaborates in Romans 8:

> Therefore, there is now no condemnation for those who are in Christ Jesus, because through Christ Jesus the law of the Spirit who gives life has set you free from the law of sin and death. For what the law was powerless to do because it was weakened by the flesh, God did by sending his own Son in the likeness of sinful flesh to be a sin offering. And so he condemned sin in the flesh, in order that the righteous requirement of the law might be fully met in us, who do not live according to the flesh but according to the Spirit. (Rom. 8:1–4)

In Galatians 2, Paul says, "I have been crucified with Christ and I no longer live, but Christ lives in me" (2:20). The believer's incorporation into the death and resurrection of Christ is another theme the apostle elaborates on in later writings, including the book of Romans: "Now if we died with Christ, we believe that we will also live with him" (Rom. 6:8). Those who follow Jesus have, in a spiritual sense, died with Him and, through His death, been released from the law. We have also, in a spiritual sense, been resurrected with Him. Now we live by faith in the Son of God (2:20), who loves us and gave Himself for us.

Paul articulates a grand theological movement in God's plan of redemption that reorients His people away from the law of Moses and toward Jesus. In the following chapters of Galatians, he will elaborate on this truth and reveal that this was God's plan all along. But first, he closes out chapter 2 with a mic-drop statement:

> [21]I do not set aside the grace of God, for if righteousness could be gained through the law, Christ died for nothing!

If it were possible to earn our own righteousness through works of the law, Jesus died in vain. Moreover, to judge believers because they aren't keeping the old covenant law—as the false teachers in Galatia were doing—is to judge Jesus Himself. It suggests that His death and resurrection weren't enough and we need to add something of our own to be truly righteous. The Judaizers were denying Christ's sufficiency. That is the dangerous false gospel Paul confronts in Galatians.

Galatians 2
Discussion Questions

1. Paul uses a lot of contentious language in Galatians. He calls the Judaizers "false believers" (2:4) and says they wanted "to make us slaves" (2:4), but "we did not give in to them for a moment" (2:5). Do you think there is an appropriate place for this confrontational posture in the modern church? How do we reconcile this approach with Peter's admonition to "Always be prepared to give an answer . . . but do this with gentleness and respect" (1 Peter 3:15)?

2. Paul admonished Peter for separating from the Gentiles in Antioch (2:11–14). Where do we see the church dividing over secondary issues, such as traditions or lifestyle choices, today? Are there any legitimate issues that would justify a division in the body of Christ (alcohol, attending same-sex weddings, marijuana, politics, etc.)?

3. One of Paul's primary points is that "a person is not justified by the works of the law, but by faith in Jesus Christ" (2:16). What works might modern Christians be tempted (consciously or subconsciously) to perform to make them a little more righteous in God's eyes? If we don't need to do these works to add to our righteousness in God's eyes, why do we do them?

Part II

PAUL,
THE THEOLOGY
PROFESSOR

FAITH OR WORKS OF THE LAW?

Galatians 3:1–14

Imagine the scene—the raised eyebrows and mutters of surprise as the orator in Galatia read that last sentence aloud: "If righteousness could be gained through the law, Christ died for nothing!" (2:21). Amid shouts of "Amen!" from the believers, the Judaizers were likely shifting in their seats and staring at their sandals. You can imagine angry comments and accusations breaking out, with the more level-headed audience members calling for order. *Brothers! Sisters! We are not yet done. Let us listen to the rest of what Paul has written before we discuss anything.*

As we move into Galatians 3, the apostle Paul dives deeper into the theological implications of the false gospel he is confronting. Let's step into Paul's classroom as he rolls up his proverbial sleeves and grabs a fresh box of dry-erase markers. Galatians is about to graduate from a letter to a master class in biblical theology. And the tone will become even more heated.

The orator continues reading as Paul unleashes a barrage of rhetorical questions:

> [1]You foolish Galatians! Who has bewitched you? Before your very eyes Jesus Christ was clearly portrayed as crucified. [2]I would like to learn just one thing from you: Did you receive the Spirit by the works of the law, or by believing what you heard? [3]Are you so foolish? After beginning by means of the Spirit, are you now trying to finish by means of the flesh? [4]Have you experienced so much in vain—if it really was in vain? [5]So again I ask, does God give you his Spirit and work miracles among you by the works of the law, or by your believing what you heard? [6]So also Abraham "believed God, and it was credited to him as righteousness."

Paul is burning with righteous anger. Here, we find one of his favorite teaching devices—the rhetorical question. He wants to snap the Galatians out of their spell and get them to shake off these bewitching teachings. Paul continues with his contrast between the works of the law and faith in Jesus. In fact, to track the case the apostle is building, let's step back and survey the contrasts he has presented over the last twelve verses of chapter 2 because he will continue to develop them throughout this letter (see Table 1).

Table 1: Paul's Contrasts in Galatians So Far

Verse	Paul contrasts . . .	With . . .
2:16	Works of the law	Faith in Jesus Christ
	Works of the law	Faith in Christ
2:19	Died to the law	Live for God
3:2	Works of the law	Believing what you heard (faith)
3:3	Means of the flesh	Means of the Spirit
3:5	Works of the law	Believing what you heard (faith)

Paul masterfully contrasts two mutually exclusive paradigms. The list on the left contains the concepts of works, law, death, and flesh, which he associates with the old covenant law. By contrast, the list on the right speaks of faith, life, the Spirit, and Jesus. The point isn't that the Sinai covenant and the law were bad or useless; Paul knows full well that they were given by God. The point is the *contrast*. As bright and helpful as a searchlight might be, it pales in comparison to the brightness of the sun. Likewise, as holy as those old covenant institutions were, they pale in comparison to the glory of the Son.

Chapter 3 begins with a fiery statement: "You foolish Galatians! Who has bewitched you? Before your very eyes Jesus Christ was clearly portrayed as crucified" (3:1). The apostle is shocked that the Galatians could have fallen for such a false gospel after he had looked them in the eye and revealed the sacrifice of Jesus to them (1:6–8). Paul has arrived at the painful heart of his problem with the Galatian believers. He probes further through a series of rhetorical questions:

> I would like to learn just one thing from you: Did you receive the Spirit by the works of the law, or by believing what you heard? Are you so foolish? After beginning by means of the Spirit, are you now trying to finish by means of the flesh? (3:2–3)

As the man who had first shared the gospel with the faith communities in Galatia, Paul's frustration is understandable. *Have you completely forgotten what happened to you?* He reminds the Galatians of when they first came to faith and how their new life in Christ began. Like a good rabbi, Paul does not merely deliver an academic lesson to his beloved pupils but engages their hearts and minds by directing them to their own personal experience. As a master apologist, Paul knows the power of rhetorical questions. He doesn't ask because he wants answers, but because the Galatians already know what the answers are.

The text shifts into the present tense: "Are you so foolish? After beginning by means of the Spirit, are you now trying to finish by means of the flesh?" (3:3). Note the contrast. The Christian life is supernatural from start to finish. We "receive the Spirit" by faith (3:2), and, as Paul will later write, we "walk by the Spirit" (5:16). Conversely, the path taught by the Judaizers sought justification "by means of the flesh" (3:3).

This is the ever-present struggle of the believer. Jesus taught us to set our minds on the things of God, not the things of man (Matt. 16:23). Paul wrote elsewhere, "Those who live according to the flesh set their minds on the things of the flesh, but those who live according to the Spirit set their minds on the things of the Spirit" (Rom. 8:5 ESV). Later in Galatians, he will contrast the "acts of the flesh" (5:19–21) with the "fruit of the Spirit" (5:22–23). This is the bumpy road every believer travels. Over time, we learn to walk by the Spirit and become more and more Christlike. The Bible calls this process *sanctification*. It is the ongoing Spirit-led process of becoming free from sin and sanctified or set apart for God.

I believe the reason we Christians are so susceptible to false "works righteousness" teachings like those of the Judaizers is because the truth just feels so scandalous. It is difficult to wrap our hearts and minds around the fact that people like us, who so often stumble and rebel and get it wrong, can be declared righteous based solely on our faith in Jesus. Such is the grace of our loving Father: "For it is by grace you have been saved, through faith—and this is not from yourselves, it is the gift of God—not by works, so that no one can boast" (Eph. 2:8–9). Amazing grace, indeed!

Notably, Paul does not accuse the Galatians of wickedness or walking in sin. Instead, he twice calls them foolish. They are sense-less, dull-witted, and irrational. Paul places the blame squarely on their lack of reasoning. They knew better, but they weren't paying attention. Consequently, they were led astray and "bewitched" (3:1) by the false teachers. Because theirs was an error of reasoning, Paul uses logical arguments peppered with rhetorical questions to correct the Galatians. He doesn't merely tell them that they are wrong;

he shows them why. Even in his exasperation, his goal is to guide them firmly and lovingly back to the truth. This is the theological discipline of apologetics at its finest.

There are two additional ideas to notice in this passage. First, Paul directly links the presence of the Holy Spirit with a genuine faith in Jesus (3:2). The Spirit, mentioned eighteen times in Galatians, plays a crucial role in Paul's defense of the gospel. In many of his other epistles, he expounds on how the presence of the Holy Spirit in a believer's life is evidence of a true conversion. Here, he reminds the believers in Galatia that there is no salvation without the work of the Holy Spirit.

Second, Paul asks the Galatians if they are "trying to finish by means of the flesh?" (3:3). Other translations (such as the ESV or the NKJV) say, "Are you now being *perfected* [or '*made perfect*'] by the flesh?" The Greek word at play is *epiteleō*, which doesn't refer to being "perfect" in the sense of "flawless." Rather, it means "finished" or "complete"; it's about fulfilling a plan or purpose. Paul is referring to justification. He is pressing the Galatians: *After being justified by faith in Jesus, are you now trying to make yourselves righteous through your own human efforts?*

The questions continue: "Have you experienced so much in vain—if it really was in vain?" (3:4). The text doesn't explicitly tell us what experiences Paul refers to. He may be speaking of the same spiritual experiences he has been trying to get the Galatians to recall. However, the Greek word behind "experiences" is *paschō*, which means "suffer." Many translations (such as the ESV) say, "Did you *suffer* so many things in vain?" (emphasis added). So, the apostle could also be speaking of a painful learning process or social ostracism because of their faith in Jesus. We are left with a mystery.

Paul continues with his indignant line of questioning: "So again I ask, does God give you his Spirit and work miracles among you by the works of the law, or by your believing what you heard?" (3:5). Professor Paul is pressing his pupils to work things out for themselves. He isn't making an academic point; he is appealing to empirical evidence from their personal experiences. God had poured out His Spirit on the Galatians and had worked miracles among them. *Did He do these things because you've been circumcised and eat kosher and keep the Sabbath? Or did these things happen because of your faith?* The Galatians knew the answer.

Now that he has their attention, Paul begins building a theological case for the proper relationship between the Christian and the law. He begins by taking his readers all the way back to the book of Genesis:

> [6]So also Abraham "believed God, and it was credited to him as righteousness."

This is a quote from Genesis 15:6. Paul raises the point that Abraham was not counted righteous based on works of the law. In fact, he lived and died centuries before the old covenant law would be given. Rather, God credited righteousness to Abraham based on his faith. He believed God.

Paul now takes his readers on a fascinating historical and theological journey, grounding his contrast between works and faith in the Torah. He draws from the stories of the Hebrew Bible, the foundational text of Jewish culture and the early church. It can be challenging for modern readers to fully appreciate this cultural context. Invoking the name "Abraham" among first-century Jews is not unlike mentioning Abraham Lincoln to Americans today. These are names that carry deep cultural connections. Both Abrahams bring to mind a tapestry of shared history, stories, images, legends, and even a national identity. For first-century Jews, however, the connection was deeply theological and far more profound.

Let's take a brief journey back to Genesis and God's covenant with Abraham to prepare us for what Paul is about to teach. He will refer to this covenant a number of times in the coming verses.

A Closer Look at the Abrahamic Covenant

Long after Abraham had become a senior citizen, the Lord made a promise to him:

> The LORD had said to Abram, "Go from your country,
> your people and your father's household to the land
> I will show you.
>
> I will make you into a great nation,
>   and I will bless you;
> I will make your name great,
>   and you will be a blessing.
> I will bless those who bless you,
>   and whoever curses you I will curse;
> and all peoples on earth
>   will be blessed through you." (Gen. 12:1–3)

Abram was seventy-five years old and childless at the time. Yet Yahweh promised that his descendants would be so numerous they would form a nation and the world would be blessed through him.[1] For several years, nothing seemed to happen. Then God again came to Abram, who had grown impatient, to reassure him of His promise:

> And Abram said, "You have given me no children; so
> a servant in my household will be my heir."
>   Then the word of the LORD came to him: "This
> man will not be your heir, but a son who is your

own flesh and blood will be your heir." He took him outside and said, "Look up at the sky and count the stars—if indeed you can count them." Then he said to him, "So shall your offspring be."

Abram believed the LORD, and he credited it to him as righteousness. (Gen. 15:3–6)

God promised Abram a son of his own flesh and that his descendants would be like the stars in the sky at night. Abram believed Him, and God credited his faith as righteousness (Gen. 15:6). This statement is teeming with theological significance. Not only is Abram's righteousness-inducing faith explicitly noted in Genesis, but it would later be alluded to in Psalm 106:31, quoted three times by the apostle Paul (Rom. 4:3, 22–24; Gal. 3:6), and once by James, the brother of Jesus (Jas. 2:23). And yet, in typical human fashion, Abram's faith later faltered.

Abram and his wife Sarah (then Sarai) grew impatient and took matters into their own hands. In a rakish scene reminiscent of a modern reality show, Sarai told Abram, "Go, sleep with my slave; perhaps I can build a family through her" (Gen. 16:2). Abram agreed, slept with her servant Hagar, and produced a son named Ishmael. Thirteen years later, God returned to the ninety-nine-year-old Abraham and promised:

Your wife Sarah will bear you a son, and you will call him Isaac. I will establish my covenant with him as an everlasting covenant for his descendants after him. (Gen. 17:19)

One year later, at the tender age of ninety, Sarah gave birth to the promised son, Isaac. In Galatians 3–4, Paul will draw heavily on this narrative. It is key to understanding the case he builds and the contrasts he makes. Ishmael was a result of Abraham's "works," while Isaac was a result of God's promise.

Galatians 3:6 serves double duty in this chapter. It is both the conclusion of Paul's opening statement and the beginning of his study of Abraham:

> 6Abraham "believed God, and it was credited to him as righteousness."
>
> 7Understand, then, that those who have faith are children of Abraham. 8Scripture foresaw that God would justify the Gentiles by faith, and announced the gospel in advance to Abraham: "All nations will be blessed through you." 9So those who rely on faith are blessed along with Abraham, the man of faith.

Paul links the faith of Abraham to Jesus so completely that he can say God "announced the gospel in advance to Abraham" (3:8). This brings to mind the enigmatic words of Jesus, who declared to the Jewish religious leaders, "Your father Abraham rejoiced at the thought of seeing my day; he saw it and was glad" (John 8:56). Paul draws a connecting line of faith that starts with Abraham, moves all the way down through the centuries to Jesus, and is extended to everyone who places their trust in Him: "Those who rely on faith are blessed along with Abraham, the man of faith" (3:9).

In other words, the blessing for "all peoples on earth" promised in Genesis 12:3 is the gospel, announced to Abraham and fulfilled in Christ. It is the salvation made available to the world through faith in Jesus. The families of the earth weren't blessed through Ishmael, the son of works. Rather, God's promise was fulfilled through Isaac, the son of faith. In fact, if you have placed your faith in Jesus, you are a living heir of the promise that Yahweh made to Abraham four thousand years ago.

Passages like this remind us why it is so valuable for Christians to spend time reading and studying our OT. Contrary to what the second-century heretic Marcion taught, Jesus did not drop down from heaven unannounced. The NT comprises the final quarter of God's grand story of redemption. And the better we know the seventy-five percent of the story that precedes it, the more we understand our beautiful Savior.

What we call the "Old Testament," Jesus called Scripture. He taught that "Everything must be fulfilled that is written about me in the Law of Moses, the Prophets and the Psalms" (Luke 24:44). To paraphrase Augustine's famous comment on the two testaments of the Christian Bible: the new is in the old concealed; the old is in the new revealed.[2] Or, as a more recent Christian thinker, Chad Bird, notes:

> The key called Christ not only opens the doors of every room from Genesis to Malachi; when you walk inside, what you see there is Christ as well. *He is the key, and he is the content.* In one way or another, every narrative, every prophet, every psalm, whispers his name and winks about his mission.[3]

The Righteous Shall Live by Faith

With the connection to Abraham established, Paul begins "stringing together pearls," as the rabbis say. In this Jewish interpretive method, often used by Jesus, various passages of Scripture are strung together in such a way that they reveal a larger truth.[4] Paul established that those who live by faith are children of Abraham (3:7) and blessed along with him (3:9). Here is the other side of that coin:

> [10]For all who rely on the works of the law are under a curse, as it is written: "Cursed is everyone who does not continue to do everything written in the Book of the Law."

The faith-based blessing of Galatians 3:9 is contrasted with the works and curses of the law in 3:10. Unlike those who live by faith, those who try to make themselves righteous through works of the law live under a curse. Paul backs up his brash statement with a quote from the Torah: "Cursed is everyone who does not continue to do everything written in the Book of the Law" (3:10). He cites Deuteronomy 27:26 to show that this isn't a new idea; it comes from the Torah itself.

Because we have already encountered the phrase "works of the law" half a dozen times in this letter, let's take a moment to examine that idea more closely.

A Closer Look at Works of the Law

At face value, the phrase "works of the law" is just what it seems: performing the duties and rituals required in the old covenant law. It is the Jewish posture of Torah observance, and Paul is not opposed to it per se. He writes elsewhere, "To those under the law I became like one under the law (though I myself am not under the law), so as to win those under the law" (1 Cor. 9:20). He does not forbid the keeping of most Mosaic rituals. In fact, Paul was happy to keep them as a means of sharing the gospel. We also see the apostle going to the temple and sponsoring believers who had taken a Nazirite vow (Acts 21:26). His "permitted but not required" position is also articulated in Colossians:

> Do not let anyone judge you by what you eat or drink, or with regard to a religious festival, a New Moon celebration or a Sabbath day. These are a shadow of the things that were to come; the reality, however, is found in Christ. (Col. 2:16–17)

Paul doesn't say, "Do not do these things," but rather, "Do not let anyone judge you" on whether you choose to keep them. He teaches that Christians should not use the observance of the Torah's prescribed days or diet as a basis for judging one's righteousness or obedience to God. He offers the same lesson to the believers in Rome:

> One person considers one day more sacred than another; another considers every day alike. Each of them should be fully convinced in their own mind. Whoever regards one day as special does so to the Lord. Whoever eats meat does so to the Lord, for they give thanks to God; and whoever abstains does so to the Lord and gives thanks to God. . . . You, then, why do you judge your brother or sister? (Rom. 14:5–6, 10)

In Galatians, Paul has made it abundantly clear why these rituals are not the basis on which we are to be judged: "A person is not justified by the works of the law, but by faith in Jesus Christ" (2:16). Believers are free to observe these things if they choose. And in the case of Jewish Christians, particularly in the first century, doing so makes all the sense in the world. In fact, Jesus anticipated that His Jewish followers would continue to observe the Sabbath (Matt. 24:20). Dr. David Rudolph, a Jewish follower of Jesus, refers to these Mosaic traditions as "boundary markers of Jewish identity."[5]

Paul's point is that those Jewish rituals must be placed in their proper perspective. They are neither forbidden nor unimportant. They are, however, secondary to faith in Jesus and contribute nothing to salvation or to the perfect righteousness of Christ that is credited to believers. Paul is not opposed to works in general. In fact, he teaches that Christians are "created in Christ Jesus to do good works, which God prepared in advance for us to do" (Eph. 2:10). Good works play a vital role in the life of a Christian, as Paul will highlight in Galatians 5–6. The issue is properly understanding what that role is.

In Galatians, Paul primarily refers to "works of the law" in the context of justification. His scope is twofold. First, he is concerned with defeating the false teachings of the Judaizers, so "works of the law" refers expressly to rituals and acts commanded under the law of Moses. We have seen two specific issues addressed so far: circumcision and food laws. The false teachers in Galatia taught that keeping these things was a requirement of righteousness. Paul argues vigorously against such a notion, and his discussion stretches beyond the black-and-white boundaries of legal obligation. He speaks as much (or more) about a spiritual posture and our orientation toward God.

Second, Paul often associates "works of the law" with an attitude of self-righteousness, boasting (4:17; 6:12–14),[6] and trying to be justified "by means of the flesh" (3:3). The works of the law are, in practical terms, works of the flesh; they can be achieved through merely human effort. Because of this, they can lead to a false sense of self-righteousness if we're not careful. As the apostle highlights in the opening verses of chapter 3, God's miraculous work among the Galatians happened through their faith and the work of the Holy Spirit, not through works of the law. The same holds true in the lives of believers today.

Galatians 3:10 says, "All who rely on the works of the law are under a curse." If we choose the law as the standard by which we want to be judged, we also choose to live under its curses for disobedience. In the Torah, Yahweh declared to the Israelites:

> See, I am setting before you today a blessing and a curse—the blessing if you obey the commands of the LORD your God that I am giving you today; the curse if you disobey the commands of the LORD your God and turn from the way that I command you today by following other gods, which you have not known. (Deut. 11:26–28)

The law of Moses served as the terms of the covenant that God made with Israel at Mount Sinai. That covenant came with both blessings and curses, which are laid out in detail in Deuteronomy 28. Paul reminds the Galatians that while God certainly promised blessings for obedience to those who lived under the law, He also vowed a very real set of curses for disobedience.

The OT records Israel's continuous inability to keep the law and honor the covenant. In fact, because Israel continually broke the covenant, Yahweh decided, in His great mercy, to make a new covenant with His people. Six hundred years before Jesus, the prophet Jeremiah wrote:

> "The days are coming," declares the LORD,
>> "when I will make a new covenant
> with the people of Israel
>> and with the people of Judah.
> It will not be like the covenant
>> I made with their ancestors
> when I took them by the hand
>> to lead them out of Egypt,
> because they broke my covenant,
>> though I was a husband to them,"
>> declares the LORD. (Jer. 31:31–32)

God is the faithful husband and Israel the unfaithful bride. It's easy to feel a sense of detachment from the ancient nation of Israel when reading these OT passages. *Boy, the people of Israel sure couldn't get their act together!* But let's be honest. We Christians today are no better at keeping God's commands. Consider just one: "Love the LORD your God with all your heart and with all your soul and with all your strength" (Deut. 6:5). Who among us can honestly say that we have been able to keep this command? *All* our heart? *All* our strength? Pursuing the law as our means of righteousness can only end in disaster. Only one Person has ever been able to keep the law perfectly—everyone else falls short (Rom. 3:23).

Paul's point in Galatians 3 is that, contrary to what the Judaizers were teaching, the law cannot justify anyone. Why? Because the curse of the law applies to anyone who breaks any of its commandments. As Paul will later argue, if we seek righteousness through even one command of the law, we are obligated to obey the whole law. He next expounds on how relying on the works of the law puts us under a curse:

> [11]Clearly no one who relies on the law is justified before God, because "the righteous will live by faith." [12]The law is not based on faith; on the contrary, it says, "The person who does these things will live by them."

Professor Paul restates his primary thesis that we are justified by faith, not by works of the law. This time, he grounds his statement in the words of the prophet Habakkuk: "The righteous person will live by his faithfulness" (Hab. 2:4). His point? These aren't new ideas. They come directly from the Hebrew Scriptures. *Even we who are Jews by birth know this.*

Paul adds, "The law is not based on faith" (3:12). He again cites the OT to show how this, too, is not a new idea: "Keep my decrees and laws, for the person who obeys them will live by them." (Lev. 18:5). The apostle draws a stark distinction: the law and faith are not the same thing. The law is based on doing; faith is based on believing. The law is about keeping; faith is about trusting. And both Habakkuk and Christ taught that eternal life is attained only through faith.

In the gospels, Jesus regularly declares (as the ESV puts it), "Your faith has made you well."[7] We never hear Him say, "Your works have made you well." When the woman who had been bleeding for twelve years touched the fringe of His garment, it was not her works but her faith that healed her.[8] Jesus forgave sins based on faith,[9] commended Gentiles for their faith,[10] and said that even faith the size of a mustard seed could accomplish amazing things.[11]

Faith is the standard that Christ set for His followers. Jesus asks in His parable of the persistent widow: "When the Son of Man comes, will he find faith on the earth?" (Luke 18:8). Jesus never declares in exasperation, "O you of little works." For Christ, and therefore for Paul, it's all about faith.

By now, even the slowest believer in Galatia would have been getting the message. Paul is practically shouting. Like a skilled teacher, he uses repetition to ensure that his pupils do not miss the point. A brief survey of just the last twenty verses reveals how often (and in how many different ways) the apostle has repeated himself on the topic of works of law:

- "A person is not justified by the works of the law" (2:16).
- "We . . . [are not justified] by the works of the law" (2:16).
- "By the works of the law no one will be justified" (2:16).
- "If righteousness could be gained through the law, Christ died for nothing" (2:21)!
- "Did you receive the Spirit by the works of the law, or by believing what you heard" (3:2)?
- "Are you now trying to finish by means of the [works of the] flesh" (3:3)?
- "Does God give you his Spirit and work miracles among you by the works of the law, or by your believing what you heard" (3:5)?
- "All who rely on the works of the law are under a curse" (3:10).
- "No one who relies on the law is justified before God" (3:11).
- "The law is not based on faith" (3:12).

I don't know about you, but I'm sensing a theme: no one is justified or saved by keeping the law. How, then, are we saved? This is the other recurring theme in those same twenty verses:

- "A person is . . . justified by . . . faith in Jesus Christ" (2:16).
- "We, too, have put our faith in Christ Jesus that we may be justified by faith in Christ" (2:16).
- "[We are] seeking to be justified in Christ" (2:17).
- "The life I now live in the body, I live by faith in the Son of God" (2:20).
- "Those who have faith are children of Abraham" (3:7).
- "Scripture foresaw that God would justify the Gentiles by faith" (3:8).
- "Those who rely on faith are blessed along with Abraham, the man of faith" (3:9).
- "The righteous will live by faith" (3:11).

The apostle Paul may be many things, but subtle is not one of them. And he is just getting started. The false teachings of the Judaizers have ignited his righteous anger. He is desperate to awaken those beloved, foolish Galatians who have fallen under their spell. *Come on, guys, you know this stuff! It's all about faith; it's always been about faith.*

The same message applies today. If we want to voluntarily keep some of the Mosaic traditions from within our freedom in Christ, that's beautiful. However, if even some small part of us thinks that keeping those things pleases God or makes us right with Him—if we believe doing so adds to our holiness or is how a righteous person should live—we are following a false gospel. Even worse, we're insulting Jesus. To believe our works are required for righteousness is to say that what Jesus did for us was nice, but it wasn't quite enough; we have to add a little something of our own to make it complete. Yet Paul couldn't be any clearer: "If righteousness could be gained through the law, Christ died for nothing!" (2:21).

The apostle continues:

> ¹³Christ redeemed us from the curse of the law by becoming a curse for us, for it is written: "Cursed is everyone who is hung on a pole." ¹⁴He redeemed us in order that the blessing given to Abraham might come to the Gentiles through Christ Jesus, so that by faith we might receive the promise of the Spirit.

The professor is guiding his pupils into deeper theological waters, all the while keeping them firmly focused on the shoreline of the OT. In the span of seven verses, Paul has cited the Hebrew Bible six times. The passage he quotes in Galatians 3:13 is particularly intriguing. He references a Torah command about capital punishment:

> If someone guilty of a capital offense is put to death and their body is exposed on a pole, you must not leave the body hanging on the pole overnight. Be sure to bury it that same day, because anyone who is hung on a pole is under God's curse. You must not desecrate the land the Lord your God is giving you as an inheritance. (Deut. 21:22–23)

Taken at face value, this passage doesn't seem to have anything to do with the crucifixion of the Messiah. However, Paul is using an ancient Hebrew method of interpretation called *midrash*.¹² This is where a rabbi pores over a text, contemplating it from every angle, and derives layers of meaning that aren't immediately obvious. Then, by "stringing pearls together," these deeper layers of meaning are linked to other texts. This process involves storytelling, homiletic expansion, and creative interpretation to a degree that would make most modern pastors and Bible scholars uncomfortable. It is a far cry from the accepted hermeneutical methods of interpretation in use today. However, because Paul was writing under the superintendence of the Holy Spirit, what was *midrash* for him has become Holy Scripture for us.

Paul links the concept of a convicted man hanging on a tree in Deuteronomy 21 to the crucifixion of Jesus to make a profound point. In the Torah, the Israelite hanging on a tree and suffering the curse of the law was the one who broke the law. In the NT, we find the negative image of that picture; it is inverted in an astonishing act of mercy. The One hanging on the tree and suffering the law's curse is the only Israelite who *never* broke the law: "Christ redeemed us from the curse of the law by becoming a curse for us" (3:13).

This is the idea theologians call *substitutionary* or *vicarious atonement*. Christ took the full punishment that we deserved for our sins as a substitute in our place. As pastor Tony Calabrese puts it, "The gospel in four words: Jesus in my place."[13] Under the law of Moses, it was the Israelites who were under a curse, not God. Jesus reversed those roles. God incarnate willingly placed Himself under a curse to free His people from that curse. New Testament scholar Ralph Martin describes it this way:

> The curse which rightfully belongs to a guilty race was voluntarily assumed by One who, although he stood outside it and was therefore blameless, chose to identify himself with our human misery and need—even to the point of being abandoned by God on the cross.[14]

Why did Jesus do this? Paul provides two reasons. First, so "the blessing given to Abraham might come to the Gentiles" (3:14). He is referring to God's promise to Abraham that "all peoples on earth will be blessed through you" (Gen. 12:3). That blessing is the gospel of Christ made available to Jews and Gentiles alike. Jesus laid down His life and willingly placed Himself under a curse in order to fulfill God's promise to Abraham. In fact, Paul often uses the Greek word *epangelia* ("promise") as shorthand for the gospel in this letter.[15]

Earlier, Paul asked rhetorically, "Did you receive the Spirit by the works of the law, or by believing what you heard?" (3:2). The tacit answer was that the Galatians had received the Spirit through faith. This brings us to the second reason Christ became a curse for us: "So that by faith we might receive the promise of the Spirit" (3:14). In His Upper Room Discourse, Jesus announced to His disciples:

> Very truly I tell you, it is for your good that I am going away.
> Unless I go away, the Advocate will not come to you; but if I go,
> I will send him to you. (John 16:7)

The Advocate, of course, is the Holy Spirit, who would not be sent until the crucified Messiah had been resurrected and the new covenant inaugurated. Paul reminds the Galatians that they have already received the Spirit. They had personally experienced the fulfillment of the Abrahamic promise. And because of the work of Jesus, the blessing of the Holy Spirit through faith is now available to "all peoples on earth" (Gen. 12:3).

Paul's statement in 3:14 that Jesus "redeemed us in order that the blessing given to Abraham might come to the Gentiles through Christ Jesus, so that by faith we might receive the promise of the Spirit" brings his argument to a triumphant conclusion. Jesus took our sentence of condemnation on Himself and secured God's promise of forgiveness for all who place their faith in Him. Paul next confronts a further objection.

THE LAW AND THE PROMISE
Galatians 3:15–29

The false teachers in Galatia seemed to be claiming that the "offspring" of Abraham were, in fact, the Jewish people. Their reasoning? God made a promise to Abraham and, centuries later, He confirmed it by making a covenant with Abraham's descendants, the Israelites. The Judaizers viewed the law as confirming or even superseding that promise. But Paul sets them straight on the true relationship between the law and the promise:

> ¹⁵Brothers and sisters, let me take an example from everyday life. Just as no one can set aside or add to a human covenant that has been duly established, so it is in this case.

The Judaizers may have been trying to convince the Galatians that because the law came after Abraham, it supplanted the Abrahamic covenant. Paul says otherwise by way of an analogy. Once a man-made agreement has been accepted and signed by all parties, you cannot simply change the terms or declare it invalid without cause. How much more does God's covenant remain binding!

Unlike the Sinai covenant, God's covenant with Abraham was unilateral. It was a one-sided agreement that required no reciprocal promise from Abraham. In fact, when that covenant was cut, God put Abraham to sleep and established it by Himself (Gen. 15). It is a divine promise carried by Yahweh alone that does not depend on human actions or conditions. Paul continues:[1]

> [16]The promises were spoken to Abraham and to his seed. Scripture does not say "and to seeds," meaning many people, but "and to your seed," meaning one person, who is Christ.

Paul narrows the scope of the Abrahamic covenant down to Jesus as the ultimate seed or "offspring" of Abraham. The Hebrew word for seed is *zera*, which can literally mean "seed" but can also refer to descendants or offspring, as it does here. The notion of Christ as *zera* predates Abraham. In fact, it harkens back to the garden of Eden and the Bible's first reference to the Messiah, which theologians call the *protoevangelium* ("first gospel"). After Adam and Eve ate the forbidden food and brought sin into the world, God promised the serpent:

> I will put enmity between you and the woman,
>   and between your offspring and her offspring [*zera*];
> he shall bruise your head,
>   and you shall bruise his heel. (Gen. 3:15 ESV)

Immediately after sin entered the world—even before Adam and Eve were cast out of the garden—God revealed His glorious plan of redemption. He foretold that Jesus, as the offspring of Eve ("being made in human likeness," Phil. 2:7), would crush the head of the enemy by defeating the sin and death that the serpent had introduced into the world. Yet He would suffer in the process. God's promises about the *zera* extend all the way back to the beginning of the human story. And they extend forward from Jesus, who is the seed from which a tree of life has sprouted that will endure until the end of time.

Paul continues to develop the relationship between God's gospel promise and the law by adding the idea of inheritance:

> [17]What I mean is this: The law, introduced 430 years later, does not set aside the covenant previously established by God and thus do away with the promise. [18]For if the inheritance depends on the law, then it no longer depends on the promise; but God in his grace gave it to Abraham through a promise.

The law of Moses did not set aside God's covenant with Abraham. The inheritance is the gospel that God promised through Abraham. And "God in his grace gave it . . . through a promise" (3:18), not through the law. The false teachers may have believed that since Abraham's descendants were given the law at Sinai, the law was now part of the package and keeping it was a requirement for inheriting the Abrahamic promises. Paul corrects the record. The addition of the law four centuries after Abraham did not void God's promise to him. From the beginning, it was Yahweh's intention that "all peoples on earth will be blessed" (Gen. 12:3) through "Abraham, the man of faith" (3:9), not through the law. We can illustrate this on a timeline (Figure 2):

The blessings God promised through Abraham bypass the law and are inherited through faith in Jesus: "For if the inheritance depends on the law, then it no longer depends on the promise" (3:18). Because this inheritance does not come by way of the Jewish law, it is not limited to Israel. It is available to "all peoples on earth" (Gen. 12:3), Jews and Gentiles alike. This truth flies in the face of the false gospel preached by the Judaizers.

Figure 2: Timeline—Abraham, Law of Moses, Jesus

430 years

Abraham   Law of Moses   Jesus

Promise   Mount Sinai   Jews & Gentiles

Blessing = Gospel (*Justification/Salvation by Faith*)

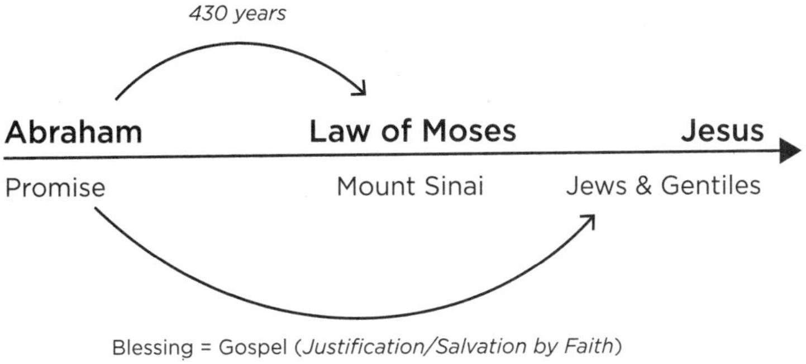

Anticipating his pupils' next question, Professor Paul asks and answers it:

> [19a]Why, then, was the law given at all? It was added because of transgressions until the Seed to whom the promise referred had come.

If the Galatians were concerned that Paul saw no value in the law, he sets them straight. The law, he says, was given for a particular purpose. With that, the apostle begins a profound exploration of the old covenant law intended to clarify its rightful role in the lives of Christians. In this verse alone, he provides three noteworthy details about the giving of the law.

First, the law was *added*. This is Paul's second reference to the law being given at a particular time in history. Earlier, he pinpointed it to 430 years after the promise to Abraham (3:17). This tells us that the law of Moses has not always existed—it had a beginning. Second, the law was added "because of transgressions" (3:19). It was given on account of sin. Paul develops this idea in more depth in Romans 5:13, where he writes, "Sin was in the world before the law was given, but sin is not charged against anyone's account where there is no law." The law was not given to help restrain the fallen nature of humanity. Rather, it was given to reveal sin and put a name on it, making wrongdoing a legal offense. Therefore, "through the law we become conscious of our sin" (Rom. 3:20).

The third major implication is found in a single word. The law was added *until* the Seed had come (3:19). The Greek preposition *achri* means the same thing as the English word "until"; it indicates the continuance of an action or condition up to a specified time. The fact that the law was added "until the Seed . . . had come" (3:19) knocks the theological legs out from under any notion that the old covenant law was still in effect. That law came with an expiration date; it ended with Christ.

A Closer Look at the Purposes of the Law

From Adam to Moses, there was no written set of standards for human beings to follow. God gave His commands directly to certain people: Adam, Noah, Abraham, Isaac, Jacob, and Moses. Our unchanging, morally perfect God certainly expressed His will in the hearts and minds of men and women at that time. But it wasn't until the covenant at Mount Sinai that He provided any sort of formalized standards.

Israel began as the clan of Jacob that went down to Egypt just seventy people strong. There, the people "increased in numbers and became so numerous that the land was filled with them" (Exod. 1:7). By the time Yahweh rescued Israel from Egypt and brought them to Mount Sinai, He was dealing with an immense group of people who had been in slavery for hundreds of years.

The law given at Sinai served at least three purposes. First, it was the terms of the Sinai covenant. If the Israelites kept the law, they would keep the covenant; if they disobeyed the law, they would break the covenant.[2] Second, the law served as a national "constitution" intended to form the Israelites into an organized nation that would serve God. It provided civil and legal guidance on how to run Israel in a way that would honor Him. Third, the law was a written moral standard. Through the law, God said to Israel, "This is what righteousness looks like for you."

In that sense, the law was a mirror. The people of Israel could metaphorically don their garments of behavior and attitudes and stand in front of the law to see how they looked. For centuries, they would be frustrated and haunted by the grimy, unkempt image that stared back at them. As Paul later explains in Romans 7, the law highlights our moral bankruptcy. It doesn't make us sinners; it reveals us to be sinners. Like a mirror, the law shows us just how far we are from God's righteous standard. In doing so, it exposes our desperate need for a savior.

At this point, many believers in Galatia listening to Paul's letter read aloud may have broken out in astonishment. *What did he just say?! Isn't the law of Moses forever? Isn't that what our Hebrew Scriptures tell us over and over again?* It may seem like a radical notion at first, but consider the "until" the law points to. It was added "until the Seed to whom the promise referred had come" (3:19). For the apostle Paul, everything in the Hebrew Scriptures points to Christ because that's what Jesus taught about Himself (Luke 24:25–49). God's promise in the garden points to Jesus

(Gen. 3:15), His promise to Abraham points to Jesus (Gen. 12:1–3), and the law points to Jesus as well.

Some have likened the law of Moses to a paramedic whose job is to stabilize injured patients and keep them alive until they reach the Physician, who brings the ultimate healing remedy. Moses knew that the law he gave to Israel was not God's last word. In fact, even as the Israelites were gathered on the plains of Moab, poised to enter the promised land with the stone tablets of the law in hand, God foretold that His people would "forsake me and break the covenant I made with them" (Deut. 31:16) And Moses prophesied to the Israelites: "The LORD your God will raise up for you a prophet like me from among you, from your fellow Israelites. You must listen to him" (Deut. 18:15). He was speaking of Christ, of course. And centuries later, on the Mount of Transfiguration, Moses and Elijah appeared alongside Jesus as the audible voice of God declared, "This is my Son, whom I love. Listen to him!" (Mark 9:7). Christ, not the law, is the master God's people now listen to.

Given that the law was a temporary addition because of sin, a word of caution is in order. As an apologist, I have seen how the conditional nature of the law of Moses can lead to confusion and even abuse. *The Ten Commandments were part of the law; have they come to an end too? Is it okay for us to murder and commit adultery now?* Antinomian groups like progressive Christianity often take this idea and run with it. They use the law's expiration date to rationalize the end of all the "antiquated" morality taught in the OT. However, they are missing a vital truth.

God's principles about right and wrong are grounded in His unchanging moral perfection. Like God, these principles had no beginning and have always been true. In fact, the law of Moses given at Sinai was not a new revelation on morality. The moral aspect of the law wasn't unique in any way. When God commands us not to murder today, it's not because of the Ten Commandments. Long before He gave Israel the law, Cain was judged for slaying his brother Abel (Gen. 4:8–16). Likewise, the stories of Sodom and Gomorrah (Gen. 19:1–29) and Joseph fleeing Potiphar's wife (Gen. 39:12–18) reveal that unfaithfulness and sexual immorality were wrong long before Sinai. The "laws" of God that define right and wrong have always been in effect.

Likewise, Yahweh's moral principles remain true long after the old covenant law completed its God-ordained mission, as Paul will discuss in Galatians 5–6. We cannot pluck the Sinai commandments out of the context in which they were given—namely, the covenant relationship between God and the ancient nation of Israel—and directly apply them to new covenant believers. The International Alliance of Messianic Congregations and Synagogues (IAMCS) is an organization of Jewish families and communities who have come to faith in Jesus as their Lord and Messiah. They offer a unique perspective on the law (Torah):

> The gift of the Torah to the Jewish people at Sinai was not revelatory in the sense of the moral aspect of it. Noah was an "ish tzadik" or "righteous man" (See Gen. 6:9); and Abraham obeyed God's statutes and commandments (Gen. 26:5), even long before the law at Sinai was even given.
>
> Torah is not a revelation of morality. Nor is the moral aspect of it unique in any way. A basic understanding of moral law is already embedded by God in the understanding of mankind. God did not appear to Israel at Sinai to present a moral code.
>
> God gave the law at Sinai, creating a unique nation. There are things given in the Torah which are unique to Israel.[3]

This is why Paul can teach, "The law is holy, and the commandment is holy, righteous and good" (Rom. 7:12) while at the same time saying that it was only binding until Christ. And he is just getting started on the "Great Until." But first, Paul makes a curious comment at the end of verse 19:

> [19b]The law was given through angels and entrusted to a mediator. [20]A mediator, however, implies more than one party; but God is one.

This is a difficult passage to interpret. The mediator Paul refers to is most likely Moses, whom God used to facilitate the Sinai covenant. The idea of angels may come from Moses speaking of "myriads of holy ones" (Deut. 33:2) in attendance at the giving of the law. Stephen, the first known Christian martyr, similarly refers to "the law that was given through angels" (Acts 7:53). The author of Hebrews also refers to the law as "the message spoken through angels" (Heb. 2:2).

Professor G. Walter Hansen suggests:

The presence of angels and the mediation of Moses in the giving of the law were understood by the Jewish people to signify the great glory of the law. But Paul argues that the giving of the law through a series of intermediaries, angels and Moses, actually demonstrates the inferiority of the law.[4]

The apostle's argument here is cryptic. He is clearly contrasting the multiple parties involved in the mediation of the law with the oneness of Yahweh. But what is his point? Paul earlier explained how the Galatian believers had already received the Spirit (3:1–5), which was the fulfillment of God's promise to Abraham (3:14). Perhaps the Judaizers were trying to convince them that they were still missing something—that only through the keeping of the rituals of the law could they fully achieve closeness with God. If so, Paul warns the Galatians otherwise.

The law, Paul says, was given through multiple layers and does not provide direct access to God. Indeed, the temple system kept individual believers at a distance from His presence. Under the old covenant law, the average Israelite was not allowed to enter the

Holy Place in the temple. Access was only available to priests. And the Most Holy Place was even more restricted, limited to one man: the high priest. By contrast, Christians are given direct access to God through the death and resurrection of Jesus (Heb. 10:19–22). There are no middlemen involved. As Paul will demonstrate in the coming verses, our relationship with God under the new covenant is far more intimate. Perhaps this is the sense in which the apostle sees the one as superior to the many.

Paul returns to his main point in the next verse:

> ²¹Is the law, therefore, opposed to the promises of God? Absolutely not! For if a law had been given that could impart life, then righteousness would certainly have come by the law.

The law does not contradict God's promises; it serves a different purpose. If the law could "impart life" (meaning eternal life, salvation), our righteousness would come through keeping it. This is a continuation of the discussion Paul began in Galatians 2:16 about justification. Here, he refers to the concept of being made right with God as "life." The implication is that God *could have* chosen to justify us through the law: "*if* a law had been given that could impart life" (3:21, emphasis added). If that were the case, "righteousness would certainly have come by the law" (3:21). Paul presents the law and the promise as mutually exclusive alternatives: righteousness cannot come through both the grace of God's promise and the keeping of the law. It's one or the other. And God chose promise. Paul continues:

> ²²But Scripture has locked up everything under the control of sin, so that what was promised, being given through faith in Jesus Christ, might be given to those who believe.

Remember that when Paul says "Scripture," he's not talking about the Christian Bible. The New Testament didn't exist at that time.

(Paul was *writing* the NT!) For Jesus and the NT authors, "Scripture" refers to the Hebrew Bible. And in this context, Paul specifically speaks of the Torah, the law. He describes it as *imprisoning* everything under sin. The Greek word is *synkleiō*, which means "confine, imprison, or enclose." It's the idea of the law being a constraining or restrictive force. This is an extension of Paul's argument that the law was given "to make wrongdoing a legal offence" (3:19 NEB).

Earlier, we discussed Paul's use of the concept of slavery in Galatians. The law imprisons us by continually reminding us of our sins without providing a way to ultimately escape them. The book of Hebrews reveals that the Torah's sin sacrifices "are an annual reminder of sins. It is impossible for the blood of bulls and goats to take away sins" (Heb. 10:3–4). They were repeated year after year as a reminder but offered no ultimate release.

Like the Israelites trapped in Egypt, the law chains us to our sin and reveals our desperate need for God to rescue us. We cannot escape on our own. In the same way that Yahweh rescued the Israelites from their Egyptian slave masters in a dramatic and unexpected fashion, He rescues us from our sin: "Christ redeemed us from the curse of the law by becoming a curse for us" (3:13). Jesus put away sin once for all by the offering of Himself (Heb. 9:26; 10:10) and, therefore, "sacrifice for sin is no longer necessary" (Heb. 10:18).

The reason the law imprisoned everything under sin was "so that what was promised, being given through faith in Jesus Christ, might be given to those who believe" (3:22). God promised Abraham, "*All peoples on earth* will be blessed through you" (Gen. 12:3, emphasis added). Yet He only gave the law of Moses to Israel. Therefore, if God's promised blessing came through the law, it would only be available to Israel. But His plan all along was to give the promise to all who believe (3:22). Accordingly, the gospel announced to Abraham (3:8) was always intended for the entire world, Jew and Gentile alike.

The law "locked up everything under the control of sin" (3:22) to point us to our need for a savior who would set us free. In this way, God's gospel promise to Abraham, fulfilled in Christ, would be given to all who place their faith in Him. Paul moves forward:

> 23Before the coming of this faith, we were held in custody under the law, locked up until the faith that was to come would be revealed. 24So the law was our guardian until Christ came that we might be justified by faith. 25Now that this faith has come, we are no longer under a guardian.

This is Paul's Great Until. He presents two concepts here. First, there is a "coming faith" in Jesus; this is the justifying faith he has been speaking of for the last two chapters. There is also the law, which he calls a "guardian." It is interesting that, although Paul says, "We were held in custody under the law" (3:23), he sees a positive aspect in it. Rather than framing the law as a harsh jailkeeper or angry dictator, he refers to it as a guardian (3:24). Other translations say "tutor" (NKJV) or "schoolmaster" (KJV). The Greek word is *paidagōgos*, which refers to a person in charge of leading and guiding children. The "custody" Paul speaks of has a protective, parental quality. Before Jesus arrived, God's people were placed under the supervision and guidance of the law. They remained so "until Christ came that we might be justified by faith" (3:24).

There is that scandalous *until* word again. The law was our guardian, but only until Christ came. This is Paul's grand theme restated yet again: we are justified through faith in Jesus, not through the law. In case his Galatian readers missed the previously implied expiration date, Paul makes himself exceedingly clear here: "Now that this faith has come, we are no longer under a guardian" (3:25). *You foolish Judaizers! We are no longer under the law.*

To paraphrase C. S. Lewis, anyone who wants to remain a sound Judaizer cannot be too careful of their reading. Paul's letter to the Galatians challenges that false theology at every turn. Now that Jesus has arrived, we are no longer under the law of Moses. This is Paul's unmistakable message to the false teachers in Galatia. It also applies to believers today who may be tempted to think that keeping the old covenant law is a requirement for following Jesus.

Paul uses a curious phrase in verse 25: "Now that this faith has come." Hasn't he been telling us that it's always been about faith? Earlier he noted that Abraham was considered righteous because of his faith (3:6). Noah, Job, David, and other OT figures were also called righteous because of their faith. However, Paul is speaking of a specific faith in this passage: faith in Christ.

The forgiveness that believers received before Jesus was ultimately based on the future death of Christ as atonement for their sins. We saw earlier that the OT animal sacrifices that atoned for sin couldn't actually take away sin. The book of Hebrews says:

> The law is only a shadow of the good things that are coming—not the realities themselves. For this reason it can never, by the same sacrifices repeated endlessly year after year, make perfect those who draw near to worship. (Heb. 10:1)

We also saw how Yahweh, in His patience, left the sins committed before the time of Jesus unpunished (Rom. 3:25). He did this so Christ could take the ultimate punishment for them on Himself at the cross. The author of Hebrews writes:

> Christ is the mediator of a new covenant, that those who are called may receive the promised eternal inheritance—now that he has died as a ransom to set them free from the sins committed under the first covenant. (Heb. 9:15)

The sacrifice of Jesus was so powerful and efficacious that it brought ultimate forgiveness even to those who had lived and sinned before He arrived! Indeed, all of Scripture—from Genesis to Revelation—is oriented toward Christ. Paul elsewhere writes this of Jesus: "From him and through him and for him are all things" (Rom. 11:36). That includes the law. Now that Jesus has come, we are no longer under that law. Paul begins to unpack what this means for believers:

> 26So in Christ Jesus you are all children of God through faith, 27for all of you who were baptized into Christ have clothed yourselves with Christ.

When we place our faith in Jesus, we become children of God "clothed . . . with Christ." This phrase refers to a change of garments. It's the idea of exchanging our dirty rags for the righteous robe of Jesus. The Father now sees us clothed in the flawless righteousness of His Son. In the previous passage (3:23–25), Paul referred to the law as a *paidagōgos*, one who leads and trains children. He is now introducing the concept of maturity into his argument against the Judaizers. In first-century Roman culture, when a child came of age, he stopped wearing his childhood garments and instead put on the *togae* (robes) of an adult. As the apostle will explain in Galatians 4, God's people have "come of age" in Jesus. We've reached a status of spiritual adulthood, so to speak. And once we've done that, why would we return to the law?

"You are *all* children of God through faith" (3:26, emphasis added). The Gentile believers in Galatia, hearing this letter read aloud, were likely beaming with joy. This was a "Welcome Home" sign confirming that they had been accepted into the Father's family with open arms and clothed in Christ through their faith. For Spirit-filled Jewish believers, this was a welcome affirmation of unity with their Gentile brothers and sisters. For the Judaizers, it was a startling splash of cold water in their faces. Paul doubles down:

> [28]There is neither Jew nor Gentile, neither slave nor free, nor is there male and female, for you are all one in Christ Jesus. [29]If you belong to Christ, then you are Abraham's seed, and heirs according to the promise.

The Jewish people are the physical seed of Abraham, his descendants by blood. This was a source of pride for many first-century Jews, including the Judaizers. In fact, many Jewish men regularly thanked God that they were not a Gentile, a woman, or a slave.[5] Paul lists these same three categories in 3:28 to upend the standard identity markers by which people are so often divided: race, social status, and gender. When it comes to joining God's new covenant people, these categories are entirely irrelevant: "In Christ Jesus you are all children of God through faith" (3:26).

This is a timely message for modern Christians living in a world so often divided along these same lines. Paul isn't saying that these categories no longer exist. There are still Jews and Gentiles, men and women, slaves and free people. But such categories have nothing to do with acceptance into God's family: "You are all one in Christ Jesus" (3:28). It's all about faith: "For God so loved the world that he gave his one and only Son, that *whoever believes* in him shall not perish but have eternal life" (John 3:16; emphasis added). The Greek word translated "whoever" is *pas*, a universal term that means "all, every." Anyone and everyone is welcome at the foot of the cross, regardless of race, gender, or station in life.

In light of this beautiful fact, Pastor Tim Keller notes that the gospel "leads to deep humility and deep confidence at the same time. It undermines both swaggering and sniveling. I cannot feel superior to anyone, and yet I have nothing to prove to anyone."[6] The book of Revelation paints a glorious picture of a multiracial, multiethnic, and multilingual body of Christ: "A great multitude that no one could count, from every nation, tribe, people and language, standing before the throne" (Rev. 7:9). The kingdom of God is diversity in unity. And the only way into that kingdom is through faith in Jesus.

In these final verses of Galatians 3, Paul picks up the concept of inheritance he introduced in 3:18. Those who belong to Christ "are Abraham's seed, and heirs according to the promise" (3:29). Earlier, the apostle had narrowed the scope of the Abrahamic promise down to Jesus, the Seed. Here, he shows how that promised gospel seed blossoms in Christ, extending to all who place their faith in Him. This concept fits comfortably in the minds of modern Christians. However, it was a revolutionary teaching for the first-century Judaizers who preached that Gentiles were required to convert to Judaism before they could follow the Jewish Messiah. Paul will continue turning their world upside down in the next chapter.

Galatians 3
Discussion Questions

1. Paul asked the Galatians, "Did you receive the Spirit by the works of the law, or by believing what you heard?" (3:2). What do you remember about your conversion experience? Have you had tangible experiences with the Holy Spirit?

2. How would you reconcile the fact that the law of Moses was temporary (3:23–25), yet God's commands about right and wrong remain? Do the Ten Commandments still apply to Christians? If so, in what way? Is the seventh-day Sabbath still required?

3. Paul says that when it comes to being adopted into God's family, our race, gender, and station in life make no difference (3:28). Where do you see the church struggling with that idea today? How diverse is your faith community—not just in terms of skin color, but also in age, political views, income, and other social factors?

CHILDREN AND HEIRS

Galatians 4:1–20

By now, the Galatians' heads were reeling. Paul has covered a lot of ground, speaking passionately about faith and the law, Jews and Gentiles, justification, and God's promise to Abraham. He has undoubtedly roused his listeners concerning the false teachers in their midst. It's not hard to imagine murmuring and hushed conversations breaking out among the audience in Galatia.

Bible translators introduced a new chapter number at this point, but the apostle's flow of thought continues uninterrupted. He has just made a somewhat surprising comment about unity. Maybe at this point, the reader looked up from Paul's letter and saw the faces of men, women, Jews, and Gentiles, sitting shoulder to shoulder and staring back at him. "You are all one in Christ Jesus . . . Abraham's seed, and heirs according to the promise" (3:28–29). By now, the Galatians may have wondered, "What is Paul trying to say?" He anticipates the question:

> 1 What I am saying is that as long as an heir is underage, he is no different from a slave, although he owns the whole estate.

> [2]The heir is subject to guardians and trustees until the time set by his father.

The apostle is developing the concept of heirs, inheritance, and coming of age. Here, he compares children and slaves. Under the civil law of that time, children were considered heirs to their father's estate. And yet, in practical terms, they were not much different than a slave. Heirs still had to obey their guardians and had no decision-making rights. Their freedom was restricted, and they didn't actually own anything. However, for heirs, all of these limitations will one day change.

For the fourth time, Paul introduces an "until" clause, applying it to his analogy of an heir. What we're seeing in Galatians is Paul, as a master teacher, restating his main themes in different ways to ensure that his readers get it. He earlier said that the law was given "until the Seed . . . had come" (3:19), "until the faith that was to come would be revealed" (3:23), and "until Christ came" (3:24). Here in the opening verses of Galatians 4, Paul restates that idea in the context of inheritance, which is not given to the heir "until the time set by his father" (4:2). All of these "untils" refer to Christ. The advent of Jesus is the central event of human history and a focal point of Paul's epistle. Christ's incarnation was the time that the Father set for His children to inherit His gospel promise.

> [3]So also, when we were underage, we were in slavery under the elemental spiritual forces of the world.

In the era before Christ, when the promises were yet to be inherited—"when we were underage"—we were in slavery to "the elemental spiritual forces of the world." This phrase is enigmatic, though it clearly has a negative connotation. Because the Galatian churches comprised both Jews and Gentiles, Paul may have chosen this particular language because it could speak to each group. Greek grammar allows for more than one interpretation.[1]

The Jewish believers might understand the phrase as a reference to basic religious teachings, the ABCs of the law of Moses. Paul has been highlighting the restrictive aspect of the law, so it makes sense that he would describe being in slavery to the ABCs of the law. At the same time, the phrase can also refer to spiritual powers, like demonic entities and evil spirits. The Gentile believers might take it as a reference to their former pagan way of life, when they worshiped idols and false gods.

> ⁴But when the set time had fully come, God sent his Son, born of a woman, born under the law, ⁵to redeem those under the law, that we might receive adoption to sonship.

This is the "until" Paul has been highlighting. Other translations (such as the ESV) use a great turn of phrase here: "when the fullness of time had come." When all of the things that God had ordained had come to pass, when the law had fully served its divine purpose—or, to use the apostle's analogy, on the date set by the Father—Jesus arrived.

Here is another profound theology lesson condensed into a single sentence: Jesus was "born of a woman, born under the law" (4:4). He was a representative of humanity as a whole and the nation of Israel in particular. We saw earlier that the law was added "because of transgressions" (3:19). While that law was only given to the people of Israel, they were certainly not the only human beings who sinned. Sin is not an Israel problem; it is a human problem. Therefore, the debt for human sin had to be paid by a human being. Paul elaborates in Romans 5, where he contrasts the sin of Adam with the righteousness of Jesus:

> Just as one trespass resulted in condemnation for all people, so also one righteous act resulted in justification and life for all

> people. For just as through the disobedience of the one man the many were made sinners, so also through the obedience of the one man the many will be made righteous. (Rom. 5:18–19)

Jesus was "born of a woman" (4:4). He is a human being, a representative before God of the entire human race. In fact, He is the promised seed of the first woman, Eve, whom Yahweh sent to crush the head of the serpent (Gen. 3:15).

Jesus is also a representative of the nation of Israel. He is the promised Jewish Messiah, the King who sits on David's eternal throne (Ps. 132:11). Six hundred years before Christ, God said of national Israel, "They broke my covenant, though I was a husband to them" (Jer. 31:32). Yahweh was a faithful husband; Israel an unfaithful bride. They were unable to keep the law and had broken the Sinai covenant. Where Israel failed, Christ succeeded. As their representative, He stepped in and kept the law perfectly, thus fulfilling it (Matt. 5:17–18).

After His resurrection, Jesus explained to His disciples that His mission had been accomplished:

> He said to them, "This is what I told you while I was still with you: Everything must be fulfilled that is written about me in the Law of Moses, the Prophets and the Psalms."
>
> Then he opened their minds so they could understand the Scriptures. He told them, "This is what is written: The Messiah will suffer and rise from the dead on the third day, and repentance for the forgiveness of sins will be preached in his name to all nations, beginning at Jerusalem. You are witnesses of these things." (Luke 24:44–48)

Jesus fulfilled His mission as both a human being and an Israelite. He was the perfect, sinless sacrifice needed to atone for our sin (1 Peter 1:19). And now, "we have been made holy through the sacrifice of the body of Jesus Christ once for all" (Heb. 10:10). By that sacrifice, Paul says, we "receive adoption to sonship" (4:5). He continues:

> ⁶Because you are his sons, God sent the Spirit of his Son into our hearts, the Spirit who calls out, *"Abba,* Father." ⁷So you are no longer a slave, but God's child; and since you are his child, God has made you also an heir.

Paul continues to explore the contrast between sonship and slavery.² God has adopted us as His children by faith and given us the privilege of addressing Him in the same intimate and unique way that Jesus did: *"Abba,* Father." We are children of the Most High King who have come of age and received our inheritance. Christ brought us the new covenant and, along with it, a paradigm shift in the way God's people relate to Him. Consider some of the momentous changes that were inaugurated at the Great Until.

When God's people were held captive under the law (3:23), they were required to make repeated, annual animal sacrifices to atone for their sin (Lev. 16). Jesus put an end to that by the "once for all" (Rom. 6:10) sacrifice of Himself: "Christ was sacrificed once to take away the sins of many" (Heb. 9:28). Therefore, unlike with the old covenant law, "sacrifice for sin is no longer necessary" (Heb. 10:18).

There has also been a significant change in our access to God's presence. In the garden of Eden, humans walked with God. Then, because of sin, we were ejected from the garden and removed from God's immediate presence. Later, at Sinai, He began the process of restoring our access to Him through His commands for a tabernacle: "Have them make a sanctuary for me, and I will dwell among them" (Exod. 25:8). Yet access to God was still restricted. A curtain separated the Most Holy Place, where Yahweh's presence dwelled, from the rest of the temple. And out of the entire nation of Israel, only one man, the high priest, was allowed to pass through the curtain. This was only allowed once each year, on the Day of Atonement.

And then, at the moment Christ died on the cross, initiating the new covenant in His blood,[3] "the curtain of the temple was torn in two from top to bottom" (Matt. 27:51). God Himself tore down the veil that was keeping His people at a distance. Unlike the Israelites under the law, followers of Jesus are free to "enter the Most Holy Place by the blood of Jesus, by a new and living way opened for us through the curtain, that is, his body" (Heb. 10:19–20). Rather than being cut off from access to God, we can now "draw near to God with a sincere heart and with the full assurance that faith brings" (Heb. 10:22).

In fact, under the new covenant, we no longer need a physical temple. The OT commanded a temple in Jerusalem. But Jesus told the Samaritan woman at the well that God's requirement of a sacred geographic location was ending:

> A time is coming when you will worship the Father neither on this mountain nor in Jerusalem. . . . A time is coming and has now come when the true worshipers will worship the Father in the Spirit and in truth. (John 4:21, 23)

The theological idea behind the temple is a sacred space where the Spirit of God dwells among His people. Because of the death and resurrection of Jesus, His Spirit dwells in believers. Christians are now God's temple: "Don't you know that you yourselves are God's temple and that God's Spirit dwells in your midst . . . for God's temple is sacred, and you together are that temple" (1 Cor. 3:16–17).

Additionally, the Levitical priesthood commanded under the law is no longer required. Every Christian is now a priest who has been given priestly duties. The apostle Peter teaches that followers of Jesus are "a holy priesthood, offering spiritual sacrifices acceptable to God through Jesus Christ" (1 Peter 2:5). The book of Revelation three times says that Jesus has made us priests of God.[4] Paul tells believers to "offer your bodies as a living sacrifice, holy and pleasing to God—this is your true and proper worship" (Rom. 12:1). That is priestly language. The duties of making sacrifices pleasing to God are now the domain of every believer in Jesus, whether Jew, Gentile, or Levite.

These are epic changes to what God had required for the fifteen centuries previous to Paul's letter to the Galatians. It's not difficult to understand the trouble that many first-century Jews had in trying to grasp the world-changing significance of Jesus, their Messiah. At the time Paul wrote this letter, the temple was still standing in Jerusalem and the Levitical priesthood was still operational. Yet the death and resurrection of Christ was the time set by the Father (4:2). His people had come of age and could now receive their inheritance by faith. And what an inheritance it is!

Consider how Paul has been framing up his contrasts so far. Let's plot his descriptions and associations on a timeline (Figure 3). The list on the right is the gospel, and everything in Scripture points to it. All roads lead to Christ.

Figure 3: Timeline—Paul's contrasts.

Abraham	Law of Moses	Jesus
Promise	Mount Sinai	Faith
Faith	Works/Flesh	Redemption
Blessings	Death	Holy Spirit
	In Custody	Freedom/Life
	Locked Up	Offspring/Seed
	Slaves/Slavery	Heirs/Inheritance
	Curses	Adoption
	Guardian/Tutor	Sons & Daughters
		Jews & Gentiles
		One in Christ

Paul draws a compelling contrast between the law and Jesus. However, a word of caution is in order. Given the picture of the law painted in Galatians, it can be tempting to dismiss it as a terrible, antiquated thing. However, the law was God's idea; it was given by Him for a holy purpose. While it's not binding on Christians today as a body of legal requirements, it still has much to teach us and is well worth our study. The law witnesses against our sin, points us to Jesus, teaches us about the heart of God and the history of His people, and is a rich source of wisdom and insight. The restrictive aspects of the law Paul writes about are undoubtedly true. But rather than diminishing our view of the law, let's let Paul's words elevate our view of Jesus. If the law was a vital part of God's holy plan, how much greater is the gospel!

Paul's Concern for the Galatians

I often wonder what kind of man Paul was. What was it like to be around him? We can glean from his writings that he was a brilliant theologian, a wise teacher, and a passionate apologist. He was also a deep thinker, well-versed in the philosophies of his day. Paul had the energy of an evangelist and the heart of a pastor. The latter aspect of his personality emerges in the following passages. First, he takes a more personal tone and appeals directly to the Galatians' experience:

> [8]Formerly, when you did not know God, you were slaves to those who by nature are not gods. [9]But now that you know God—or rather are known by God—how is it that you are turning back to those weak and miserable forces? Do you wish to be enslaved by them all over again?

This passage has led to some debate among Bible scholars as to the intended audience. Phrases like "when you did not know

God" (4:8) and "turning back to those weak and miserable forces" (4:9) suggest that Paul is addressing his comments to the Gentiles in Galatia. However, he doesn't clearly signal this shift in audience. In the previous passage, he said that God sent His Son "to redeem those under the law" (4:5), a phrase that would primarily apply to Jews, though it could also include God-fearing Gentile proselytes.[5]

Based on the verses that follow, Paul seems to be continuing to cast a wide net with his comments, targeting both Jewish and Gentile believers. Now that they have come to faith in Christ, he wonders how they can turn back to those "weak and miserable forces" (4:9). Whether he means the ABCs of the law or pagan spiritual powers, the apostle asks, "Do you wish to be enslaved by them all over again?" (4:9). Who is your master? Those former things or Christ?

Next, we find another clue about what the false teachers promoted:

> [10]You are observing special days and months and seasons and years! [11]I fear for you, that somehow I have wasted my efforts on you.

This is a curious comment. Similar to Paul's earlier reference to "elemental spiritual forces" (4:3), this remark could be equally applied to Jewish and Gentile believers. As much as we wish Paul had provided more detail, you have to wonder if he intentionally kept this statement ambiguous for a reason. He could be thinking of the many festivals and celebrations observed in the pagan world. However, in light of his ongoing argument against the teachings of the Judaizers, it's equally likely he is referring to the Jewish liturgical calendar with its sabbaths, new moons, and feasts.

In Galatians 2 we discovered that the Judaizers were teaching circumcision as a requirement. Paul's rebuke of Peter in Antioch further revealed that keeping the Jewish food laws was part of their false doctrine. And his comment here about "observing special days and months and seasons and years" (4:10) suggests that the Judaizers were also teaching observance of the Torah's appointed times. Because the Galatian Christians were starting to believe that they needed to keep those special days, the apostle sarcastically wonders if he has wasted his efforts on them (4:11). Paul is concerned that the Galatians might end up rejecting the gospel entirely, so he reminds them of their shared history. Notice the blend of love and frustration in his tone. Paul is writing as a loving, spiritual father:

> [12]I plead with you, brothers and sisters, become like me, for I became like you. You did me no wrong.

Paul's appeal to "become like me" is a bit of a mystery. The apostle frequently urged his readers in his letters to imitate him in the sense that he was imitating Christ through loving service and sacrifice for the sake of the gospel.[6] But this is different. Paul exhorts them to "become like me, for I became like you" (4:12). The NEB renders it, "Put yourselves in my place . . . for I have put myself in yours." Given the intensity of Paul's focus on the false teachers thus far, I tend to agree with Bible commentator H. D. Betz that Paul likely means something more direct: "I have become like a Gentile for your sake—are you now going to Judaize?"[7]

Perhaps sensing the intensity of his argument, Paul shifts gears and adopts a warmer tone. He addresses the Galatians as his wayward yet beloved flock. Here, we learn a little backstory about what originally brought Paul to Galatia:

> [13]As you know, it was because of an illness that I first preached the gospel to you, [14]and even though my illness was a trial to you, you did not treat me with contempt or scorn. Instead, you welcomed me as if I were an angel of God, as if I were Christ Jesus himself.

Many of the Galatian believers who were gathered to hear this letter read aloud likely knew exactly what Paul was referring to. Evidently, his original intention was not to preach the gospel in Galatia. He was forced into it by illness. However, Paul doesn't state what he was struggling with. The two most popular theories are either malaria or trouble with his eyesight. More important than the nature of the illness is what it led to. A health problem caused the apostle to wander off his intended path and landed him in Galatia. And what does he do while being nursed back to health? He preaches the gospel and ends up starting a collection of churches.

Paul addresses the Galatians at the heart level, reminding them of his love for them and their love for him: "Even though my illness was a trial to you . . . you welcomed me as if I were an angel of God" (4:14). There was once genuine affection between Paul and the believers in Galatia:

> ¹⁵Where, then, is your blessing of me now? I can testify that, if you could have done so, you would have torn out your eyes and given them to me. ¹⁶Have I now become your enemy by telling you the truth?

Paul expresses a sense of personal betrayal. *At one time, you would've sacrificed anything for me. What happened to that love?* He directs them back to when he first shared the gospel with them and they received the Holy Spirit by believing what they heard (3:2). Many of those listening to this letter likely felt warm memories stirring. This isn't some unknown teacher writing to them; it's their old friend *Paulus*. He appeals to their personal relationship to remind them that he is an honest man telling them the truth about the false teachers leading them astray. And about those false teachers:

> [17]Those people are zealous to win you over, but for no good. What they want is to alienate you from us, so that you may have zeal for them.

I like how *The Message* paraphrases this verse: "They want to shut you out of the free world of God's grace so that you will always depend on them for approval and direction, making them feel important." In contrast, godly teachers don't "use people" or lay unnecessary burdens on them. They don't promote zeal for themselves but for God by helping others grow in the knowledge, freedom, and love of Jesus, who taught, "My yoke is easy and my burden is light" (Matt. 11:30).

We learn something important from Paul's apologetic focus in this passage. A telltale sign of false teachers is their emphasis on converting people to their own agenda rather than preaching submission to the truth and fullness of Christ. When it comes to Christian teachers, a great litmus test is to ask yourself if they are promoting zeal for themselves and their ministry or for Jesus Christ. We find this insidious deception across the spectrum of false theologies we encounter today. For example, in progressive Christianity the ethic of "inclusion" is often elevated to the highest value. And while inclusion is a beautiful, biblical ethic (anyone can come to the cross!), its reverence above all other biblical values leads to what Dietrich Bonhoeffer called *cheap grace*: "The preaching of forgiveness without requiring repentance . . . absolution without personal confession."[8]

Cheap grace is found in movements like The Reformation Project (TRP), which describes itself as a Bible-based Christian organization seeking to advance LGBTQ inclusion in the church. TRP argues, "The arc of Scripture points toward inclusion, not exclusion,"[9] and promotes the value of integrating sexual "others" into the Christian church. We can certainly affirm that the gospel of Christ is for everyone, including the members of the LGBTQ community. They are made in God's image and, therefore, are worthy of dignity and love. They absolutely should be welcomed into our church communities. We desperately want them to know Christ and be adopted into God's family as our brothers and sisters.

At the same time, joining God's family means acknowledging that the "family rules" apply equally to everyone and are there for our benefit. This is true for all of His adopted children—gay, straight, or other. As the saying goes, "God loves us just as we are. But He loves us too much to leave us there." To place our faith in Christ is to submit to His authority over every area of our lives and let Him change us into His image. (Which is no easy feat, no matter who we are or what we struggle with!) However, TRP teaches that the Bible's sexual prohibitions don't apply to Christians today because they are "grounded in cultural concerns about patriarchal gender roles," which the New Testament points us beyond.[10] Like the Judaizers of Paul's day, their ultimate focus is not on submitting to Christ and making Him known, but on advancing their own social agenda.

On the other end of the spectrum, we find hairsplitting moralizers and modern-day Judaizers who revere the rule of law as the highest value. This kind of legalism values conduct over mercy. For example, the theology of Seventh-Day Adventism (SDA) teaches that the dividing line between true followers of God and followers of the devil is what day of the week they worship. SDA founder Ellen G. White wrote:

> When you obey the decree that commands you to cease from labor on Sunday and worship God, while you know that there is not a word in the Bible showing Sunday to be other than a common working day, you consent to receive the mark of the beast and refuse the seal of God.[11]

SDA is not a theology focused on Christ but on human conduct. It teaches that if you do not keep the seventh-day Sabbath, you will receive the mark of the beast. Not only is this idea unbiblical, but it also causes SDAs to focus on converting people to their Sabbath agenda more than pointing them to the saving gospel of Jesus. The same is true of many "Torah-observant" Christian sects, who claim (just like the false teachers in Galatia) that believers are required to keep the old covenant law.

It is a sad reality that the mission field for groups like SDA, Hebrew Roots, progressive Christianity, and others is the church. Rather than sharing the gospel with those who do not yet know Jesus, these groups evangelize believing Christians, hoping to convert them to their agenda. This is the "danger from within" that Paul warned of. This "other agenda" is what he called "a different gospel—which is really no gospel at all" (1:6–7). It is a counterfeit gospel because it points away from Jesus.

Legalists often make the mistake of believing that the commands of God are where life is found. Yet life is not found in the law but in Jesus, who said:

> You study the Scriptures diligently because you think that in them you have eternal life. These are the very Scriptures that testify about me, yet you refuse to come to me to have life. (John 5:39–40)

For Jesus and the NT authors, the "Scriptures" were the Hebrew Bible (OT). Jesus says the law, the prophets, and the writings are not where life is found. Rather, they were given to bear witness about Him. Christ alone is the source of eternal life.

While legalism and progressivism occupy opposite ends of the theological spectrum, they make the same error, namely, diminishing the fullness of Jesus by focusing on something other than Him. Therefore, the solution is the same for both; return to a focus on the person and work of Christ. That is precisely what Paul does in this letter.

Think about how this played out in Galatia. Paul visited the Galatians, led them to Christ, and started new churches. The Judaizers later arrived on the scene, and they weren't trying to win lost sinners to Jesus but seeking to lure saved believers away from Him. Consequently, the false teachers in Galatia were poaching converts from the gospel-believing churches that the apostle had planted. This is a sad irony. In contrast, Paul's motivation is to glorify Jesus. As he'll later write, "May I never boast except in the cross of our Lord Jesus Christ" (6:14). Conversely, the motivation of the Judaizers was "that you may have zeal for them" (4:17).

Paul warns the Galatians to beware of any teacher who insists that works of the law are how we are made right with God. The Judaizers thought doing so made them more pious and righteous in God's eyes. They further believed that not doing those works was sinful and a basis for exclusion from the faith community. These are all lies that undermine the sufficiency of Christ. Notice the fruit of those false teachings: the theology of the Judaizers was leading to shame, confusion, and division in the body of Christ. This is a far cry from the fruit of the Holy Spirit that Paul will discuss in the next chapter. He continues:

> [18]It is fine to be zealous, provided the purpose is good, and to be so always, not just when I am with you. [19]My dear children, for whom I am again in the pains of childbirth until Christ is formed in you, [20]how I wish I could be with you now and change my tone, because I am perplexed about you!

This is the concern of a pastor, a rebuke in love. Paul is contending for the souls of his young flock. He uses the same term of affection for the Galatians that he does for the church in Corinth and for Timothy and Titus: "My dear children." Paul's love for the believers in Galatia drives him to take such a firm tone and tell them the hard truth. They had become sons and daughters of God and heirs through faith in Christ (4:6–7), but the Judaizers were trying to turn them back into beggars and slaves. Bible teacher Warren Wiersbe describes the situation well:

> They had not lost the *experience* of salvation—they were still Christians; but they were losing the *enjoyment* of their salvation and finding satisfaction in their works instead. Sad to say, *they did not realize their losses.* They actually thought they were becoming better Christians by substituting Law for grace, and the religious deeds of the flesh for the fruit of the Spirit.[12]

With that, Paul moves from grace back to truth and from the concerned pastor to the stern spiritual teacher, rebuking his beloved students with another profound lesson from the life of Abraham.

THE ALLEGORY OF
SARAH AND HAGAR
Galatians 4:21–31

e~ও

It's easy to imagine the apostle Paul with a Torah scroll next to him opened to the Book of Genesis as he wrote his epistle to the Galatians. He keeps returning to the life of Abraham in his argument against the Judaizers. The Hebrew word *torah* means "instruction or teaching," and the redemptive history we find in Abraham's story is every bit as much *torah* as the legal commands given at Sinai. Paul is masterfully using the Torah to refute the misapplication of the Torah by the false teachers in Galatia.

This letter gives us a sense of the apostle as a scholarly student of Scripture. Elsewhere, he reveals that he "studied under Gamaliel and was thoroughly trained in the law of our ancestors" (Acts 22:3).[1] He was also "of the tribe of Benjamin, a Hebrew of Hebrews; in regard to the law, a Pharisee" (Phil. 3:5). Paul knew his stuff. Yet, to our modern sensibilities, what he does next in Galatians 4 might seem a little sketchy. He will again utilize the Jewish interpretive technique of *midrash* by applying elements of the story of Abraham,

Sarah, and Hagar to his teaching about Christians and the law. We may wonder how he felt comfortable taking such license with an OT text and using it to teach something the original human author almost certainly did not intend. But his contemporary readers would not have batted an eye. *Midrash* was a common technique among Jewish rabbis and sages. Paul's approach to it, however, is uniquely Christian.

The NT authors regularly used events outside of the Hebrew Bible as their starting point for interpreting it. They viewed the OT in light of the life, death, resurrection, and ascension of Jesus, which scholars call the "Christ event." Jesus had opened their minds to what the law and the prophets foretold about him.[2] That was the fundamental reality by which they interpreted their Hebrew Scriptures. Their experiential knowledge of Jesus as the promised Messiah and God incarnate became their hermeneutical priority. Professor Keith Stanglin puts it this way:

> With Jesus's help, early Christian hindsight became twenty-twenty. Thus the experience of the Christ event was sufficient to lead the early church to see their Jewish Scriptures in a whole new light.[3]

This phenomenon is what scholars call *sensus plenior*, the "fuller sense." Theologian Donald Hagner explains this concept:

> Given the fulfillment that has come to God's people in Jesus Christ, the Old Testament is seen to possess a fuller or deeper sense, a *sensus plenior* . . . The first Christians, all of them Jews, read their (Old Testament) Scriptures differently after they had encountered the risen Christ and the fulfillment he brought. From that time on, Christ was the hermeneutical key that unlocked the meaning of the Old Testament—their interpretation became Christocentric.[4]

Said another way, the OT authors unconsciously (yet guided by the Holy Spirit) alluded to things beyond the horizon of their knowledge. Some of the things they wrote, or at least the deeper meaning behind their words, wouldn't be fully revealed until Christ. *Sensus plenior* is a perspective that can only be seen from the other side of the cross. The Hebrew Bible looks forward to the coming of a promised Messiah who would arrive at some point in the distant future. But unlike the NT authors, the OT authors didn't know who it would be or when He would come. The apostle Peter captures how intently the prophets looked for the coming Christ:

> Concerning this salvation, the prophets, who spoke of the grace that was to come to you, searched intently and with the greatest care, trying to find out the time and circumstances to which the Spirit of Christ in them was pointing . . . They spoke of the things that have now been told you by those who have preached the gospel to you by the Holy Spirit sent from heaven. Even angels long to look into these things. (1 Peter 1:10–11, 12)

Conversely, Paul is writing to the Galatians some twenty years after Jesus's resurrection. By the time he composed this epistle, God had revealed who the Messiah would be and when He would come. What the OT prophets saw as a mystery of the future had become a known fact in the present age for Paul and the NT authors. So, we can think of the NT as an inspired commentary on the OT. This is Scripture interpreting itself.

With that, let's read through Paul's provocative allegory as a whole. Then, we'll circle back and unpack it verse by verse.

> [21]Tell me, you who want to be under the law, are you not aware of what the law says? [22]For it is written that Abraham had two sons, one by the slave woman and the other by the free woman. [23]His son by the slave woman was born according to

the flesh, but his son by the free woman was born as the result of a divine promise.

24These things are being taken figuratively: The women represent two covenants. One covenant is from Mount Sinai and bears children who are to be slaves: This is Hagar. 25Now Hagar stands for Mount Sinai in Arabia and corresponds to the present city of Jerusalem, because she is in slavery with her children. 26But the Jerusalem that is above is free, and she is our mother. 27For it is written:

"Be glad, barren woman,
    you who never bore a child;
shout for joy and cry aloud,
    you who were never in labor;
because more are the children of the desolate woman
    than of her who has a husband."

28Now you, brothers and sisters, like Isaac, are children of promise. 29At that time the son born according to the flesh persecuted the son born by the power of the Spirit. It is the same now. 30But what does Scripture say? "Get rid of the slave woman and her son, for the slave woman's son will never share in the inheritance with the free woman's son." 31Therefore, brothers and sisters, we are not children of the slave woman, but of the free woman.

This is a densely packed passage. What Paul is doing here, and he states it outright, is presenting an allegory. He uses characters and events from the book of Genesis to symbolically teach biblical truth. To make sure we fully understand the details of this allegory, let's take a moment to revisit the specific events Paul references in the life of Abraham. And if you've ever been tempted to think of the Bible as boring, check out this scandalous tale.

A Closer Look at Abraham, Sarah, & Hagar

Earlier, we saw how God promised Abraham that he would have many descendants: "I will make you into a great nation" (Gen. 12:2). After more than ten years of waiting, Abraham and his wife Sarah, still childless, grew impatient and took matters into their own hands.[5] At Sarah's insistence, Abraham slept with her servant, Hagar, and bore him a son, Ishmael. Paul's allegory picks up a few additional details about this story that we don't want to miss.

Genesis 16:4 says, "When [Hagar] knew she was pregnant, she began to despise her mistress." Hagar, a foreigner and a slave, was the first to give Abraham a son. As the first mother in the family, she began to view Sarah with contempt. She was forced to have Abraham's child because of Sarah's barrenness. *You can't even give your own husband children!* This, in turn, caused Sarah to resent Hagar. She complained to Abraham, "You are responsible for the wrong I am suffering. I put my slave in your arms, and now that she knows she is pregnant, she despises me" (Gen. 16:5).

Sarah ended up treating Hagar so harshly that she ran away. But God came to Hagar in the wilderness and sent her back to Abraham, promising He would take care of her and the baby. So, she returned and gave birth to Ishmael. Thirteen years later, Yahweh came to Abraham and reminded him of His promise of a son by his wife, Sarah. This would be the son through whom blessings would come to all the peoples of the earth. Abraham responded by falling on his face in disbelief. "He laughed and said to himself, 'Will a son be born to a man a hundred years old? Will Sarah bear a child at the age of ninety?'" (Gen. 17:17). God's response? He told Abraham to call this son Isaac, a name that means "one who laughs." For the rest of Abraham's life, his son, "One Who Laughs," would be a living, ever-present reminder that God's promises never fail.

The birth of Isaac created a new problem. Ishmael had been Abraham's only son for fourteen years. When baby Isaac arrived, Ishmael became jealous. Here, we find an example of the apostle's use of *midrash* to creatively interpret the OT story. The text of Genesis simply says, "Sarah saw that the son whom Hagar the Egyptian had borne to Abraham was *mocking*" (Gen. 21:9, emphasis added; some translations such as the ESV say "laughing.")[6] Paul expounds on this text, describing Ishmael as "persecut[ing]" Isaac (v. 29) and causing trouble in the home. So, Sarah told Abraham to cast out the slave woman and her son, which broke Abraham's heart:

> But God said to him, "Do not be so distressed about the boy and your slave woman. Listen to whatever Sarah tells you, because it is through Isaac that your offspring will be reckoned. I will make the son of the slave into a nation also, because he is your offspring." (Gen. 21:12–13)

Abraham obeyed, packing up provisions and sending them away. And as Hagar and Ishmael wandered in the wilderness, God came to them and cared for them (Gen. 21:17–20).

With that drama in mind, let's work through Paul's allegory. He begins by asking the Galatians, "You who want to be under the law, are you not aware of what the law says?" (4:21). Those tempted to follow the teachings of the Judaizers and put themselves back under the law seemed to be forgetting that "all who rely on the works of the law are under a curse" (3:10). With that, Paul launches into the story of Abraham, Sarah, and Hagar, applying it to their contemporary situation.

Notice how he introduces the two women: "For it is written that Abraham had two sons, one by the slave woman and the other by the free woman" (4:22). Paul reiterates his pervasive contrast between slavery and freedom, this time dressing it up in the figures of Hagar (the servant) and Sarah (Abraham's freely chosen wife). In fact, in this allegory we are going to find a reiteration of all the contrasts we cataloged back in Table 1.[7]

Paul adds, "His son by the slave woman was born according to the flesh, but his son by the free woman was born as the result of a divine promise" (4:23). When the apostle describes Ishmael as "born according to the flesh," he is not speaking of the physical aspect of his birth. Both sons were born the same way in that respect. Rather, he is drawing a contrast. In this passage, Paul uses the Greek word *sarx* ("flesh") to refer to sinful human nature. Yahweh had promised Abraham a son, but in their impatience and doubt Sarah and Abraham chose to do things their own way. Rather than trusting God's promise, they resorted to works of the flesh. By contrast, Isaac was born of Sarah, just as God had promised. Thus, Ishmael was born according to the flesh, while Isaac was born according to God's promise.

Paul continues:

These things are being taken figuratively: The women represent two covenants. One covenant is from Mount Sinai and bears children who are to be slaves: This is Hagar. (4:24)

Biblical authors rarely explain their allegories and parables, so this is a welcome revelation. Paul plainly states that his allegory is about two covenants: the old covenant made at Sinai and the new covenant inaugurated by Jesus. Hagar represents the old covenant, which "bears children who are to be slaves." The imagery is clear and, for the Judaizers, startling. The old covenant law bears children into slavery. Paul adds another layer to his allegory of Hagar:

> Now Hagar stands for Mount Sinai in Arabia and corresponds to the present city of Jerusalem, because she is in slavery with her children. But the Jerusalem that is above is free, and she is our mother. (4:25–26)

The plot thickens. Hagar "stands for Mount Sinai." She represents the old covenant and its law in this allegory. She also symbolizes the present-day (for Paul) Jerusalem. It's not hard to imagine murmurs of protest breaking out among the listeners in Galatia as these verses were read aloud. For them, Jerusalem was Zion, the active epicenter of the Jewish faith. The temple still stood and was fully operational. Jews still made a pilgrimage to Jerusalem three times every year for the feasts. Synagogues throughout the world were built so that they faced Jerusalem. Yet Paul describes that vibrant, sacred city as "in slavery with her children" (4:25).

Just twenty years before Paul wrote Galatians, Jesus foretold that Jerusalem would cease to be the epicenter of worship (John 4:21–24). Under the new covenant, the formal worship of God was no longer restricted to a geographic location; it was now to take place "in the Spirit and in truth" (John 4:24). What Jesus prophesied came to pass, and Paul says Hagar symbolizes "the present city of Jerusalem, because she is in slavery with her children" (4:25).

In first-century Roman culture, children born to slaves were also slaves unless the master adopted them into his family. Just as Hagar was a slave and her son Ishmael was born a slave, the present

Jerusalem is in slavery with *her* children. Paul is speaking of his fellow Jews who had refused the gift of grace that God offered them through Jesus and were still under the slavery of the law. By contrast, "The Jerusalem that is above is free, and she is our mother" (4:26).

Paul then quotes from the prophet Isaiah:

For it is written:

> "Be glad, barren woman,
>   you who never bore a child;
> shout for joy and cry aloud,
>   you who were never in labor;
> because more are the children of the desolate woman
>   than of her who has a husband."
>   (4:27, quoting Isaiah 54:1)

Unless we are particularly familiar with the book of Isaiah, Paul's use of this quote is puzzling. He is using another classic rabbinic technique called *remez*, which means "hint." This is where a teacher quotes only a part of a verse, knowing that those students familiar with the passage will fill in the rest. Jesus did this often. It's not unlike saying, "What goes up . . ." and leaving your listener to complete the thought. (This is why I always say that the more familiar we are with our OT, the more NT goodness we will discover.)[8]

Paul quotes the opening verse of Isaiah 54, where the prophet personifies Jerusalem as a woman barren and bereaved of children. Many of Paul's readers will recognize this as a chapter that speaks of the future glory of Israel. Isaiah goes on to tell the barren woman (Jerusalem), "You will spread out to the right and to the left; your descendants will dispossess nations" (Isa. 54:3). Paul invokes Isaiah 54 to remind his readers that God can bring abundant blessing where, humanly speaking, it seems impossible. This is the same principle behind Isaac being miraculously born to a barren ninety-year-old Sarah. Paul connects this same idea to Gentile believers who miraculously become heirs of God's promises to Abraham through faith.

More directly, "the present city of Jerusalem" in slavery is contrasted with the "Jerusalem that is above," which is free. The apostle contrasts the "old Jerusalem" with what the book of Revelation calls the "new Jerusalem," the messianic kingdom. Bible scholar Alan Cole elaborates:

> The concept of a 'new Jerusalem' is very familiar from the Old Testament . . . in view of passages like Ezekiel 48 and Isaiah 62, it was easy to speak of an ideal Jerusalem already existing in heaven in the mind and purpose of God, and one day destined to be established on earth by the act of God. . . . To Paul, 'the present Jerusalem' . . . is not only the familiar city of his boyhood, with the temple at its heart, but also the whole race of Israel. Again, this was a familiar usage from the Old Testament, where 'Jerusalem' can stand for its inhabitants or even for the whole nation.[9]

In Paul's allegory, the "present city of Jerusalem" (4:25) symbolizes the old covenant. The "Jerusalem that is above" (4:26) represents the new covenant. He includes a curious phrase regarding the Jerusalem above. She is not only free, but "she is our mother" (4:26). This idea, too, is drawn from Isaiah 54, which speaks of a mother who seems barren but whose descendants will one day be so numerous that they dispossess nations. Paul's point? Mothers give life, the law does not (3:21). Life is found only in Christ. In this allegory, life comes through Sarah, who represents the new covenant with its freedom and promise. By contrast, the Judaizers want to cling to the slave woman Hagar (the old covenant and its law) as their source of life. In doing so, they were enslaving every Christian they converted to their false theology. To see the relationships at play and the stark contrast Paul is drawing, an illustration may be helpful (Figure 4):

Figure 4: Diagram of Paul's allegory in Galatians 4:21–31.

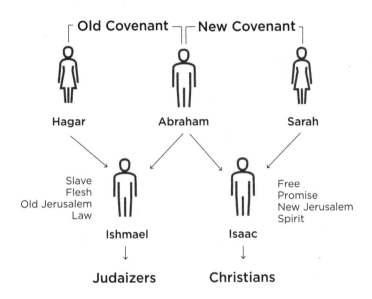

Warren Wiersbe draws out several fascinating parallels in Paul's allegory.[10] In the same way the law was "added" (3:19) after the promise, Sarah (the free woman) was Abraham's wife first, and Hagar (the slave) was added as his second wife. In God's kingdom, grace and promise come before the law. This goes all the way back to the garden of Eden, where Yahweh showed grace at the first sin and promised to one day set things right (Gen. 3:15) before he issued the curses to the man and woman. Likewise, by His grace, God rescued Israel out of Egypt before He gave them the law.

Abraham's marriage to Hagar was the byproduct of unbelief and a work of the flesh. It's the oldest story in the book: Abraham and Sarah didn't trust God and chose to go their own way. They enlisted Hagar to do what only Sarah could do, but it failed. Paul's allegory brilliantly summarizes what he has been teaching for the last two chapters: the law was never intended to be our source of life, justification, or spiritual inheritance.

Paul next brings the allegory home for the Galatians:

> Now you, brothers and sisters, like Isaac, are children of promise.
> At that time the son born according to the flesh persecuted the
> son born by the power of the Spirit. It is the same now. (4:28–29)

In the same way that Ishmael mocked his little brother Isaac and caused turmoil in the home, the Judaizers were causing unrest in Galatia with their false gospel. The struggle for fidelity to God's Word felt so acutely in Galatia continues today. Christ's church is under attack from within. Whether it's progressive Christianity, Jehovah's Witnesses, Mormonism, SDA, Torahism, or any other belief system not "in line with the truth of the gospel" (2:14), the biggest threat comes from those who claim faith in Jesus but do not have Christ at the center of their theology.

In light of these modern controversies, Paul's counsel to the churches in Galatia is sobering. He prescribes the same remedy that Abraham used with Ishmael:

> But what does Scripture say? "Get rid of the slave woman and her
> son, for the slave woman's son will never share in the inheritance
> with the free woman's son." Therefore, brothers and sisters, we
> are not children of the slave woman, but of the free woman.
> (4:30–31)

Christians are children of the free woman, not the slave woman. "If you belong to Christ, then you are Abraham's seed, and heirs according to the promise" (3:29). Paul doesn't view the pursuit of justification through law-keeping as a secondary issue of religious preference. This isn't an "agree to disagree" matter. He calls it a perversion of the gospel of Christ (1:7) and "not . . . in line with the truth of the gospel" (2:14). This is a salvation matter. And because the stakes are so high, Paul quotes Genesis 21:10 to declare that just as God cast out Hagar, the churches in Galatia ought to purge the Judaizers from their midst.

This is the same remedy Paul prescribed for the sexual immorality running rampant in the church in Corinth. He likened it to yeast and wrote:

> Don't you know that a little yeast leavens the whole batch of dough? Get rid of the old yeast, so that you may be a new unleavened batch—as you really are. (1 Cor. 5:6–7)

There are certain teachings that, if allowed to spread throughout the church unchecked, will catch on and ultimately undermine the gospel of Christ.

According to our modern chapter numbering, this brings us to the close of chapter 4. However, an argument could be made that Paul's thought is actually concluded in the next verse, which says, "For freedom Christ has set us free; stand firm therefore, and do not submit again to a yoke of slavery" (5:1 ESV).

Oh foolish Galatians! Christ has set you free. How can you submit again to slavery?

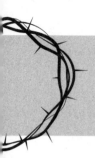

Galatians 4
Discussion Questions

1. Many of us have dealt with a Mormon ringing the doorbell or a Jehovah's Witness handing out a *Watchtower* journal. But false teachers often aren't always so easily identifiable. Sometimes they look just like us and go to the church just down the road. What are some ways we can tell if what they are sharing is true and biblical? How can we test their teachings?

2. Why does Paul say that Jesus was "born of a woman, born under the law" (4:4)? What significance does that have for the gospel?

3. Does it make you uncomfortable that Paul took creative license with the OT text to create his allegory of Sarah and Hagar? When teaching truths about God, what do you believe is the proper role of allegory and storytelling? What are the dangers of these kinds of teaching devices?

Part III

PAUL, THE CONCERNED PASTOR

FREEDOM IN CHRIST
Galatians 5:1–12

༃

The allegory of Abraham, Sarah, and Hagar surely ruffled some feathers in Galatia. Here, again, it's easy to imagine the assembly breaking out in heated conversation over what they just heard. *Paul is right! We need to cast those false teachers out from among us!* Maybe the Judaizers in attendance tried to double down on their denunciation of Paul. *He's not even a real apostle! Did you hear what he just said about Jerusalem? Don't listen to him.*

And yet, over the last four chapters, Paul has systematically dismantled the Judaizers' arguments. They argued that circumcision was required for anyone who wanted to follow the Jewish Messiah, but Paul showed how even James, Peter, and John agreed that circumcision was not required of believers (2:1–10). The false teachers painted Paul as a preacher gone rogue, but the apostle revealed that, in reality, he was called by God and given the "right hand of fellowship" (2:9) by the other apostles in Jerusalem.

The Judaizers urged Jewish believers to separate from Gentiles who didn't eat kosher, but Paul confronted Peter and publicly exposed why breaking fellowship over food was "not acting in line with the truth of the gospel" (2:14). The false teachers claimed we are made right with God by keeping the law, but Paul revealed that no one can be justified by the law; justification comes only by faith in Jesus (2:16). He pointed to Abraham to validate that the gospel has always been about faith (3:6). He further showed that "if righteousness could be gained through the law, Christ died for nothing!" (2:21) and, further still, declared that "all who rely on the works of the law are under a curse" (3:10).

The Judaizers taught that the law of Moses superseded God's promise to Abraham, but Paul established that "if the inheritance depends on the law, then it no longer depends on the promise; but God in his grace gave it to Abraham through a promise" (3:18). The false teachers also taught that the law was eternal and our source of eternal life, but the apostle showed why the law cannot impart life (3:21–22) and how it was given to point us to the Great Until: the arrival of the promised Christ (3:23–25).

The false teachers taught that the physical descendants of Abraham were heirs to God's promises, but Paul revealed how the promises were actually given to *all* who believe: "If you belong to Christ, then you are Abraham's seed, and heirs according to the promise" (3:29). The Judaizers argued for the obligation of the old covenant law, but Paul revealed that the law "bears children who are to be slaves" (4:24). In fact, the apostle's allegory of the women and the two covenants was the *coup de grace* for the false teachers, showing that followers of Jesus "are not children of the slave woman, but of the free woman" (4:31).

Yet, as both a master apologist and a concerned pastor, Paul knows that it's not enough to tear down false theology. Errant teachings need to be replaced with sound, biblical understanding. As we move into chapter 5, he shifts toward showing the Galatians what the true gospel should look like in our lives. While sustaining his argument against the false teachers, Paul now begins to focus on the practical application of the gospel.

Paul's thoughts in these final two chapters follow a logical sequence. Before we work through the text, it will be helpful to contrast the path he is going to describe for Spirit-led Christians with the path he has already traced for works-focused Judaizers. Both begin with being set free by faith in Christ, but they end in very different places.

Paul will argue that Spirit-led Christians are no longer under bondage to the law because we've been set free by Christ (5:1). However, we're not to abuse our freedom but rather "walk by the Spirit" (5:16). When we let the Spirit guide us, He awakens a desire in us to love and live for others rather than for ourselves. We begin to see the fruit of the Spirit in our lives (5:22–23), which leads us to good works. And because this life of freedom is so meaningful, we want to live it for God's glory (6:14). Our eyes become focused outward on God and others, and our path leads to freedom.

Conversely, consider the path of the false teachers in Galatia. It is the same track followed by modern Christians who have fallen into works-righteousness. (A direction many of us are prone to drift if we're not careful!) This path starts with good intentions. We understand that the commandments were given by God and want to keep them to show our love and obedience. As we do so, we sense that we are becoming more spiritual and feel closer to God. We begin noticing progress; we're not doing some of the things we used to do. The people around us are starting to notice, as well, and even compliment us on our obedience and spiritual discipline. We sense that God sees it too. Notice that our focus has begun shifting ever so subtly from the work of Christ to our own works.

Somewhere along the way, we begin measuring our spiritual progress by how well we are keeping the commandments. Before we know it, and often without realizing it, we are walking by the flesh, living out our faith under our own human effort rather than by the Spirit. Those practicing works-righteousness inevitably begin to notice those around them who are "weaker in faith" and aren't keeping the old covenant rituals and commands with the same consistency. So, they try to convince their weaker brothers to follow their path and leave their sinful, lawless ways behind. That way, these weaker brothers can learn to please God and be righteous before Him the way the Judaizers are. Their eyes are now focused inward on themselves, and their path leads to slavery (see Figure 5).

Figure 5: Two paths for walking out our faith in Jesus

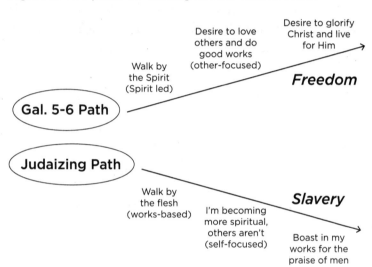

The difference is striking. The path Paul will describe in Galatians 5–6 starts with faith and leads to freedom and the glorification of God. The road of works-righteousness starts with works and leads to slavery and self-glorification. Paul warned the Galatians that the false teachers want to "alienate you from us, so that you may have zeal for them" (4:17). They sought their own glory and longed to be recognized as pious and obedient. Obeying God, of course, is essential; it is what He expects of us. As I heard one pastor say, obedience is God's "love language." However, the Judaizers were not only obeying for the wrong reasons, but they were also living out their new covenant obedience in entirely the wrong way.

The Judaizers argued that Paul's doctrine of grace was dangerous. This is the same claim we hear from moralizers and works-righteousness teachers today: if we do away with the rules and rituals, we will end up walking in sin and disobedience. They are rightly sounding a warning bell against antinomianism. Yet, as the apostle will explain in the first half of chapter 5, they are missing the whole point of freedom in Christ.

The same verse that summarized Paul's allegory of Sarah and Hagar introduces his next thought:

> ¹It is for freedom that Christ has set us free. Stand firm, then, and do not let yourselves be burdened again by a yoke of slavery.
>
> ²Mark my words! I, Paul, tell you that if you let yourselves be circumcised, Christ will be of no value to you at all. ³Again I declare to every man who lets himself be circumcised that he is obligated to obey the whole law. ⁴You who are trying to be justified by the law have been alienated from Christ; you have fallen away from grace. ⁵For through the Spirit we eagerly await by faith the righteousness for which we hope. ⁶For in Christ Jesus neither circumcision nor uncircumcision has any value. The only thing that counts is faith expressing itself through love.

Everything Professor Paul taught in the previous two chapters has led up to this glorious statement: "It is for freedom that Christ has set us free." Faith in Jesus frees us from the law and its attendant curses. The apostle urges the believers in Galatia not to follow the Judaizers back into keeping the old covenant law, which he calls a "yoke of slavery" (5:1).

The imagery of a "yoke" carries a double-edged meaning in Scripture. In Jewish tradition, the idea of a yoke could take on a positive sense, such as describing the teachings or guidance of a rabbi. Jesus said:

> Take my yoke upon you and learn from me, for I am gentle and
> humble in heart, and you will find rest for your souls. For my
> yoke is easy and my burden is light. (Matt. 11:29–30)

Here, "yoke" carries the idea of tethering yourself to a wise
teacher. At the same time, a yoke can symbolize an oppressive burden such as servitude or slavery. For example, when the Israelites
were in bondage in Egypt, Yahweh declared, "I am the LORD,
and I will bring you out from under the yoke of the Egyptians"
(Exod. 6:6).[1]

In the NT, the apostle Peter uses this same imagery to describe
the law. During the debate at the Jerusalem Council, "some of the
believers who belonged to the party of the Pharisees stood up and
said, 'The Gentiles must be circumcised and required to keep the
law of Moses'" (Acts 15:5). Peter responded, "Why do you try to
test God by putting on the necks of Gentiles a yoke that neither we
nor our ancestors have been able to bear?" (Acts 15:10). He agrees
with Paul regarding the obligation of the old covenant law for new
covenant Christians.

In the opening verses of Galatians 5, Paul appropriates the
imagery of a yoke to show that, under Jesus, the law that guarded
and guided us also chains us to our sin. He says, "Mark my words!"
(5:2). The Greek interjection means, "Behold! Take note!" It's like
a modern pastor saying, "All eyes up here!" After speaking broadly
of the law, Paul homes in on one aspect.

"I, Paul, tell you"—he attaches every ounce of his apostolic
authority to the statement that follows—"that if you let yourselves
be circumcised, Christ will be of no value to you at all" (5:2). The
apostle is not referring to the medical procedure per se, but ritual
circumcision as commanded under Moses as a means of making
oneself right with God. This is an enormous statement, because
circumcision was one of the most significant aspects of identity for
God's covenant people. To make sure we appreciate the full weight

of the argument Paul is about to make, let's take a brief look at the history of circumcision in the Torah.

A Closer Look at Circumcision in the Torah

The rite of circumcision is introduced twice in the OT. First, after declaring Abraham righteous because of his faith (Gen. 15:6), God gave him the rite of circumcision as a sign of the covenant (Gen. 17:1–14). At the same time that Yahweh changed his name from Abram ("exalted father") to Abraham ("father of many"), He required the patriarch to mark the very part of his body that he would use to enter fatherhood. Teacher Tim Mackie describes a remarkable pattern in the signs God assigns to His covenants.[2]

The sign of God's covenant with Noah was the rainbow. His covenant promise to never again flood the Earth is inseparably connected to the very rain He used to flood it. The rainbow reminds us of both the terror of His divine judgment that destroyed every living creature on Earth and the beauty of His divine mercy that promises, "Never again will there be a flood to destroy the earth" (Gen. 9:11).

Likewise, the sign of God's covenant with Abraham was circumcision. The cutting off of Abraham's foreskin is a reminder of his lack of faith in God's promise and his misuse of the Egyptian slave Hagar with that same part of his body. It is an act of judgment. However, circumcision is also a sign of mercy. God did not cut off Abraham from His promise but instead commanded him to mark the very part of his body that contained the future promise of the seed.

Just a few years after Paul wrote to the Galatians, he

explained the connection between righteousness and circumcision in greater detail in his letter to the Romans. He describes Abraham as the father of both the uncircumcised (Gentile believers) and the circumcised (Jews):

> We have been saying that Abraham's faith was credited to him as righteousness. Under what circumstances was it credited? Was it after he was circumcised, or before? It was not after, but before! And he received circumcision as a sign, a seal of the righteousness that he had by faith while he was still uncircumcised. So then, he is the father of all who believe but have not been circumcised, in order that righteousness might be credited to them. And he is then also the father of the circumcised who not only are circumcised but who also follow in the footsteps of the faith that our father Abraham had before he was circumcised. (Romans 4:9–12)

Circumcision was first introduced in the Torah as a sign of the righteousness credited to Abraham because of his faith. But the ritual did not make him righteous; Abraham was declared righteous *before* he was circumcised. Centuries later, at Sinai, circumcision was reintroduced and given additional significance. Under the law of Moses, this rite also included a commitment to the Sinai covenant and an obligation to keep its law.

Here is where things get interesting. The Judaizers stressed circumcision as a requirement, and, indeed, it was required under the law (Lev. 12:1–4). This was not just for Israelite males; it was even required of Gentiles who were sojourning with Israel and wanted to partake in feasts like Passover: "No uncircumcised male may eat it" (Exod. 12:48). This ritual was essential to life and faith under the Sinai covenant. And yet, under the new covenant, neither Paul nor the other apostles required circumcision (2:1-5). This ritual was clearly not an obligation for followers of Jesus.[3] Why?

In our closer examination of Peter and kosher food (see pp. 69-74), we saw that Israel was called to be holy (Hebrew: *qadosh*) and set apart for God under the old covenant. He declared, "I have set you apart from the nations to be my own" (Lev. 20:26). God did so through a number of commands unique to Israel, including the circumcision of males. The Lord did not require this ritual of any Gentile nation. Circumcision was a visible marker that indicated Israel was "cut off" from the rest of the world, so to speak, and belonged to Yahweh. Because of the work of Jesus, the purpose for this distinction in the flesh ended with the new covenant. Paul wrote earlier, "There is neither Jew nor Gentile . . . for you are all one in Christ Jesus" (3:28). There is no longer a need to distinguish Jews from Gentiles. He put it this way in Romans:

> This righteousness is given through faith in Jesus Christ to all who believe. There is no difference between Jew and Gentile, for all have sinned and fall short of the glory of God, and all are justified freely by his grace through the redemption that came by Christ Jesus. (Rom. 3:22-24)

Ephesians 2 further explains how faith in Jesus brought an end to the barrier between Jews and Gentiles:

> For he himself is our peace, who has made the two groups one and has destroyed the barrier, the dividing wall of hostility, by setting aside in his flesh the law with its commands and regulations. His purpose was to create in himself one new humanity out of the two, thus making peace, and in one body to reconcile both of them to God through the cross, by which he put to death their hostility. (Eph. 2:14–16)

Jesus "[set] aside . . . the law with its commands and regulations" (Eph. 2:15). This sentiment is even stronger in the Greek: Jesus *katargeō* the law, which means "causing something to come to an end or to be no longer in existence, abolish, wipe out, set aside."[4] The Mosaic rituals, including circumcision, are not a requirement for followers of Jesus.

To the astonishment of the Judaizers, Paul's reprimand about circumcision revealed that things had changed dramatically. Circumcision was a requirement under Moses. Yet Paul doesn't simply say it is no longer required. He says those who now accept that procedure as a Mosaic ritual undermine the value of what Jesus did for us: "If you let yourselves be circumcised, Christ will be of no value to you at all" (5:2). Ritual circumcision was a sign of the Sinai covenant, and undergoing that rite represents an attempt to seek justification before God through works of the law: "Every man who lets himself be circumcised . . . is obligated to obey the whole law" (5:3).

Paul has spent the previous four chapters of Galatians preaching that the law is not how we are made right with God. He has spoken of the law in terms of slavery, imprisonment, and curses and declared its expiration date at the Great Until. The apostle's declaration is unmistakable: we are living in a new era and under a new covenant. Because of the death and resurrection of Jesus, things have changed substantially. The Judaizers were acting like they never got the memo. They continued to preach the keeping of the whole law, and Paul labors to disabuse them of that notion:

> You who are trying to be justified by the law have been alienated from Christ; you have fallen away from grace. (5:4)

The NIV tames Paul's passionate language in this verse and, in doing so, misses a literary wink. Rather than "alienated," other translations (such as the ESV) say, "you are *severed* from Christ" (emphasis added). This is a clever wordplay on the idea of circumcision. It's the same Greek word used in the Ephesians 2 passage we just read: *katargeō*, "abolish, set aside, wipe out." In the Sermon on the Mount, Jesus famously said that He did not come to abolish (*katargeō*) the law and the prophets but to fulfill them (Matt. 5:17). Here in Galatians 5, we find the inverse; in trying to be justified by keeping the law, the Judaizers are abolishing Christ.

The law and faith are mutually exclusive paths to being declared righteous by God. Paul has made this point several times already. Justification does not come through a combination of law and faith. It's not "mostly this" and "a little of that." The *one and only way* we can be declared righteous in God's eyes is through faith in Jesus. Paul continues:

> For through the Spirit we eagerly await by faith the righteousness for which we hope. For in Christ Jesus neither circumcision nor uncircumcision has any value. The only thing that counts is faith expressing itself through love. (5:5–6)

Here is another compelling use of contrast. In the middle of a passage critical of a work of the flesh (circumcision), Paul points us to the Spirit and faith: "Through the Spirit we eagerly await by faith" (5:5). When we live by faith, we depend on the Spirit. When we seek righteousness under the law, we are relying on our flesh, our own works.

Through the Spirit and faith, we eagerly await "the righteousness for which we hope" (5:5). And, by the way, the Greek word *elpis* ("hope") doesn't contain the wishful uncertainty of the English word. *Elpis* is a confident expectation. Elsewhere, Paul refers to "Christ Jesus our hope (*elpis*)" (1 Tim. 1:1) and "the hope (*elpis*) stored up for you in heaven" (Col. 1:5). Here in 5:5, he is likely referring to the final consummation of our righteousness at the end of our life when our eternal salvation is realized.

The apostle pulls no punches in his comment on the old covenant ritual of circumcision. This is a law that he and his Jewish ancestors had observed for fifteen long centuries. It's no wonder the false teachers in Galatia were having trouble accepting the new covenant reality. Paul speaks as plainly as possible: "In Christ Jesus neither circumcision nor uncircumcision has any value" (5:6). Neither status offers any benefit, nor adds an iota to our righteousness in God's sight.

In fact, to undertake circumcision as a ritual would be to put ourselves under the code of Moses and obligate us to keep the entire law. And if we do that, we have also put ourselves back under the curse of the law (3:13). "No!" Paul says: "Do not let yourselves be burdened again by a yoke of slavery" (5:1). The Galatians who were being swayed by the Judaizers may not have seen this connection. Likewise, Christians today who preach "Torah observance" are also missing this fact. Paul makes it painfully obvious. For those in Christ, what counts is not circumcision or any other ritual or work of the law. What matters is "faith expressing itself through love" (5:6).

Here we find another fascinating turn of phrase. When Paul talks about faith "expressing itself" through love, he uses the Greek root word *ergon*, meaning "works or deeds." This is the same Greek word he used earlier to stress that "a person is not justified by *ergon*, but by faith in Jesus Christ" (2:16). For this reason, other translations of 5:6 (such as the ESV) say that what counts is "faith *working* through love." What matters is faith *ergon* through love: a faith with hands and feet. Paul is not talking about simply believing that Jesus is real and ending the story there. Biblical faith is more than mental assent to a fact. The faith Jesus and the NT authors speak of is a heart commitment—a loyalty and trust resulting in action, a faith that expresses itself through love.

In other words, Paul is not opposed to good works. In fact, in the apostle's famous passage teaching that salvation comes by grace through faith alone, he also speaks of doing good works:

> For by grace you have been saved through faith. And this is not your own doing; it is the gift of God, not a result of works, so that no one may boast. For we are his workmanship, created in Christ Jesus *for good works*, which God prepared beforehand, that we should walk in them. (Eph. 2:8–10 ESV, emphasis added)

Good works are the result of faith; they testify that it is genuine. Said another way, authentic faith in Christ results in a changed life that reflects what He taught us to do: love one another, serve one another, forgive, be generous, and so on. In the parable of the sheep and goats, Jesus reveals how true faith expresses itself through love:

> Then the righteous will answer him, "Lord, when did we see you hungry and feed you, or thirsty and give you something to drink? When did we see you a stranger and invite you in, or needing clothes and clothe you? When did we see you sick or in prison and go to visit you?"
>
> The King will reply, "Truly I tell you, whatever you did for one of the least of these brothers and sisters of mine, you did for me." (Matt. 25:37–40)

Faith working through love feeds the hungry, welcomes strangers, clothes the poor, and visits prisoners. Notice that the righteous didn't say, "Lord, we have been circumcised." And in Mark 10, Jesus did not say, "Whoever wants to become great among you must be circumcised." In fact, Jesus nowhere commands us to observe such rituals. How does He say we become great in the kingdom of God?

> Whoever wants to become great among you must be your servant, and whoever wants to be first must be slave of all. For even the Son of Man did not come to be served, but to serve, and to give his life as a ransom for many. (Mark 10:43–45)

Paul is not arguing that circumcision is a bad thing in and of itself. In fact, he is willing to keep some of the old covenant rituals himself for the sake of the gospel (1 Cor. 9:19–23). But they are not the focus of a Christ-centered life. Those rituals are not what Jesus commanded of His followers, nor what makes us righteous. Faith is the only way we can be declared righteous in God's eyes. And a genuine faith expresses itself through love for others.

This why Paul, a circumcised Jewish man, can write, "For in Christ Jesus neither circumcision nor uncircumcision means anything, but faith working through love" (5:6 LSB). He will repeat this theme several more times in this letter: the only thing that counts is faith, and it's a faith that works through love.

Paul continues:

> 7You were running a good race. Who cut in on you to keep you from obeying the truth? 8That kind of persuasion does not come from the one who calls you. 9"A little yeast works through the whole batch of dough."

The Galatians were doing great, running a good race. But then something happened. Paul asks rhetorically, "Who cut in on you to keep you from obeying the truth?" He and his readers know exactly to whom he is referring. The Judaizers' teaching that Christians are required to keep the works of the law isn't merely a distraction or a waste of time. It is a falsehood that knocks believers off course and hinders them from obeying the truth!

Paul categorizes this aberrant teaching as a deceptive persuasion that "does not come from the one who calls you" (5:8); it comes from among you. "A little yeast works through the whole batch of dough" (5:9). The apostle uses this same analogy when he later admonishes the church in Corinth for the sexual immorality among them: "Don't you know that a little yeast leavens the whole batch of dough?" (1 Cor. 5:6). The Galatians need to get rid of the bad yeast before it ruins the whole loaf. The Judaizers are a dangerous influence that threatens to spread throughout the entire community if they're not dealt with. A little bad theology can ruin the whole gospel. Paul continues:

> [10]I am confident in the Lord that you will take no other view. The one who is throwing you into confusion, whoever that may be, will have to pay the penalty.

This is strong language. Those trying to convince the Galatians that righteousness is found in the works of the law are committing a crime against God and will pay a penalty. *Make no mistake, God's justice will catch up to the false teachers trying to lure you away to their counterfeit gospel.*

> [11]Brothers and sisters, if I am still preaching circumcision, why am I still being persecuted? In that case the offense of the cross has been abolished.

There is some debate over Paul's meaning in this verse. Some scholars suggest that the Judaizers may have been spreading rumors about Paul preaching circumcision. Indeed, Paul had Timothy circumcised before preaching to the Jews in Lystra and Iconium because he didn't want anything getting in the way of the gospel (Acts 16:1–3). This was standard operating procedure for the apostle. For the sake of the gospel, he became all things to all people:

> To the Jews I became like a Jew, to win the Jews. To those under the law I became like one under the law (though I myself am not under the law), so as to win those under the law. To those not having the law I became like one not having the law (though I am not free from God's law but am under Christ's law), so as to win those not having the law . . . I do all this for the sake of the gospel, that I may share in its blessings. (1 Cor. 9:20–21, 23)

It's no surprise there was some confusion about what Paul was teaching. In certain scenarios, he may have looked like a practicing Jew, even though he did not consider himself under the law. The most straightforward interpretation of his question, "If I am still preaching circumcision, why am I still being persecuted?" (5:11) is that if Paul were still preaching circumcision, as he did before he met Jesus, the Judaizers would have no problem with him. "In that case the offense of the cross has been removed" (5:11 ESV).

Notice the source of offense isn't Paul or even circumcision. It's the cross of Christ. The false teachers wouldn't have been so bent out of shape if Paul had taught faith in Jesus in *addition* to the old covenant law. But they found the exclusivity of the cross objectionable. The cross declares that Christ is all-sufficient. Jesus Himself proclaimed, "I am the way and the truth and the life. No one comes to the Father except through me" (John 14:6). The apostle Peter also declared, "Salvation is found in no one else, for there is no other name under heaven given to mankind by which we must be saved" (Acts 4:12). Not even God's holy law can save. Salvation is the work of Christ alone.

Consequently, Paul is offended and angry that the Judaizers are denying the gospel:

> ¹²As for those agitators, I wish they would go the whole way and emasculate themselves!

My goodness. Paul does not want to be misunderstood. The Greek word for "emasculate" is *apokoptō*, which means "cut off," as in castrated. Paul wishes those who preach circumcision would just cut the whole thing off! What he loses in sensitivity, he gains in clarity. This imagery plays on the idea of how, in the Torah, circumcision was a cutting rite that stood for the idea of being cut off or set apart from the world for God.

The apostle Paul knows that those who preach circumcision as a ritual of righteousness are putting themselves under the bondage of the law and turning their backs on their freedom in Christ. So, he repeats his warning that like bad yeast, like the slave woman and her son, and like an overzealous circumcision (pick your metaphor), the Judaizers must be cut off from the believers in Galatia before their false gospel spreads.

LIFE BY THE SPIRIT

Galatians 5:13–25

Paul now addresses those on the other side of the road from legalism. He knows the temptation to abuse the principle of "faith alone" can be strong for his readers, including us today. We can swing the pendulum so far in the opposite direction that we end up in just as much trouble. This is the danger of antinomianism (lawlessness), which says that, at the end of the day, it doesn't really matter whether we live a virtuous life as long as we have faith. Although we might not think of it in such stark terms, that attitude can sometimes arise in the shadowy corners of our hearts: *As long as I've prayed and asked Jesus into my heart, I'm good. I don't really need to read my Bible, do the whole church thing, or try to follow Jesus.*

Lawlessness can creep into the life of any believer. At some level, we all struggle with the temptation to abuse our freedom. It can be hard to detect because it's almost always couched in the language of freedom and grace. The error is so subtle that we often find it in our hearts without realizing how it got there. Paul offers a corrective for those who might misunderstand or distort what he says about Christians not being under the law. He heads off this faulty line of reasoning by explaining the proper use of our freedom in Christ:

> ¹³You, my brothers and sisters, were called to be free. But do not use your freedom to indulge the flesh; rather, serve one another humbly in love.

We have been called to freedom, Paul says, but don't think that translates into license to do whatever we want. We tend to view freedom as a lack of rules, responsibilities, and obligations. It's often linked to financial freedom. We think if we were rich, we could be truly free. We wouldn't have to "work for the man" or play by society's rules: we could come and go as we please, travel wherever and whenever we want, and eat at the fanciest restaurants. There would be no limits for us!

Yet the headlines are littered with lottery winners whose new-found "freedom" ended up destroying their lives. Take, for example, Billy Bob Harrell Jr., who won the Texas Lottery jackpot of $31 million in 1997. He quit his Home Depot job, bought a ranch, and made massive donations to his church. Within a year, this faithful believer split with his wife. "Just 20 months after winning the lotto, Harrell was broke and took his life, putting a shotgun to his chest and pulling the trigger."[1] According to the *Dallas Observer*, Harrell confided to a financial adviser shortly before his death, "Winning the lottery is the worst thing that ever happened to me."[2]

Jesus did not set us free from the law in the sense that we no longer have moral obligations. He didn't release us from our responsibility to obey Him. The fact that Christians are no longer under the law does not mean that we are now free to sin; it means we're now free *from* sin. The law chained us to our sin and offered no avenue of escape. This is why it required sin sacrifices to be continually repeated year after year.[3] The law was a guardian that could not release us from our sin, but only remind us of it (Heb. 10:1–4). As Paul wrote earlier, "Now that this faith [in Jesus] has come, we are no longer under a guardian" (Gal. 3:25). Christ freed us from the law with his "once for all" sacrifice, but we still serve God. In his letter to the Romans, Paul wrote:

> But now, by dying to what once bound us, we have been released from the law so that we serve in the new way of the Spirit, and not in the old way of the written code. (Rom. 7:6)

Believers are called to live lives of obedience and "serve one another humbly in love" (5:13). Jesus commanded, "As I have loved you, so you must love one another" (John 13:34). He taught the kind of self-sacrificial, other-focused love that "enslaves" us to one another in the highest sense of freedom. Paul said the faith that saves and justifies us "is faith expressing itself through love" (5:6). Therefore, freedom in Christ does not lead to license but to love.

Paul's discussion of faith and works up to this point often raises a question. The apostle earlier said, "A person is not justified by the works of the law, but by faith in Jesus Christ" (2:16). Yet, in this verse (and following), he talks about the priority of serving others, doing good, and avoiding certain sinful behaviors. Aren't these things considered works? And doesn't the apostle James tell us that "faith apart from works is dead" (James 2:26 ESV)? Let's take a moment to address this common point of confusion on the relationship between faith and good works.

A Closer Look at Faith and Works

The NT consistently teaches salvation by faith alone.[4] Galatians has historically played a major role in that issue, which, as we've seen, was at the heart of the Reformation. However, Bible-reading believers are often confused by a passage in the book of James. Some even claim James contradicts Paul on this issue. The confusion is understandable. Taken at face value, both apostles seem to be saying opposite things. Paul says, "A person is not justified by the works of the law, but by faith" (2:16). James says, "You see that a person is justified by works and not by faith alone" (James 2:24 ESV).[5] What's going on here?

Like the English word *justify*, the Greek word it translates (*dikaioō*) has different meanings, which are determined by the context in which it is used. The apparent contradiction arises because of a lack of context. Most English dictionaries offer at least two primary meanings for the word *justify*:

1. To prove or show to be just, right, or reasonable (ex., "trying to *justify* his selfish behavior")
2. To judge, regard, or treat as righteous and worthy of salvation (ex., "God *justifies* through faith in Christ")[6]

These two definitions of "justify" also apply to the Greek word *dikaioō*.[7] Paul and James use the same word in different senses. In Galatians 2:16, Paul uses the second definition: "A person is not *dikaioō* (declared righteous and worthy of salvation) by the works of the law, but by faith." James, on the other hand, uses the first definition: "You see that a person is *dikaioō* (proven or shown to be right) by what they do and not by faith alone" (James 2:24). He is not speaking of declaring someone righteous in a legal sense but about proving something right. How do we know James uses *dikaioō* in this way? Look at the OT example he uses to make his point.

James asks, "Was not Abraham our father justified by works when he offered up his son Isaac on the altar?" (James 2:21 ESV). He is referring to Genesis 22, where Abraham proved his faith through his willingness to sacrifice his son. This event happened decades *after* God had already declared Abraham righteous because of his faith (Gen. 15:6). So when James says Abraham was "justified by works when he offered up his son" (James 2:21 ESV), he's not saying Abraham was declared righteous and worthy of salvation by doing so. He means Abraham's obedience to such a grievous command proved the genuineness of his faith. Abraham justified himself as a faithful follower of Yahweh through his obedience.

When read in context, James 2:14–26 reveals that he is talking about the same kind of "faith expressing itself through love" that Paul teaches in Galatians 5:6. When we come to a genuine faith in Jesus, the Holy Spirit dwells in us and empowers us to do good works. We saw earlier that believers were "created in Christ Jesus to do good works" (Eph. 2:10). James teaches that if we claim to have faith but our lives show no outward evidence of it, our faith is lifeless: "Faith by itself, if it is not accompanied by action, is dead" (James 2:17). True faith expresses itself through love for God and others. Good works are evidence of a saving faith, not a prerequisite for salvation.

Professor Bruce Gore makes the profound observation that love fulfills everything the law requires.[8] If you think about it, the law sets minimum limits for how we should behave: don't kill, don't steal, don't commit adultery. Legalists get caught up in defining those limits. *If I don't claim this on my taxes, is that stealing? Am I really killing someone if I'm only mad at them? Is it really adultery if it's just an emotional affair?*

Love isn't concerned with such boundaries. Rather, the biblical love Jesus modeled for us takes a sacrificial posture focused outward on others. It's not worried about where the line is drawn for stealing, cheating, or harming others. Biblical love focuses on giving generously, which is the opposite of stealing, and on commitment and honesty, the inverse of cheating. It is concerned with building up others and speaking life to them, the antithesis of hating and killing.

In other words, biblical love is not content with simply avoiding wrongdoing; it is compelled to actively engage in "rightdoing." Believers who walk by the Spirit will invariably exceed the minimum standard of the law. This is why, immediately after exhorting his readers to use their freedom in Christ to "serve one another humbly in love" (5:13), Paul can conclude:

> ¹⁴For the entire law is fulfilled in keeping this one command: "Love your neighbor as yourself."

The entire law is fulfilled. Let that sink in for a moment. If we love others with true sacrificial, biblical love, we have fulfilled all that the law requires. Paul is repeating what he learned from Jesus: our two greatest mandates are to love God and love our neighbor (Matt. 22:37–39). "All the Law and the Prophets hang on these two commandments" (Matt. 22:40). This is what new covenant obedience looks like. The heart of the law is fulfilled without the need for circumcision, dietary restrictions, feasts, or other old covenant rituals. In light of this biblical mandate, Paul goes on to warn the Galatians:

> ¹⁵If you bite and devour each other, watch out or you will be destroyed by each other.

Earlier, we looked at two paths for walking out our faith in Jesus (Figure 2, page 85). The Spirit-led path leads to the glorification of God, but the way of the Judaizers leads to the glorification of themselves. Although the false teachers may have begun with a genuine desire to faithfully obey God, their path inevitably leads to a prideful heart. We humans are all too prone to boast about ourselves rather than the Lord. And that false pride can lead even faith communities to "bite and devour each other" (5:15).

The same danger that Paul saw in the churches in Galatia still exists today. And it's not a Christian problem; it's a human problem. In the world, it is very easy to get pulled into a comparison game, focusing on whether we're more virtuous and worthy than the next person. This attitude has no place in the body of Christ. It only leads to division. Paul offers the antidote:

> [16]So I say, walk by the Spirit, and you will not gratify the desires of the flesh. [17]For the flesh desires what is contrary to the Spirit, and the Spirit what is contrary to the flesh. They are in conflict with each other, so that you are not to do whatever you want. [18]But if you are led by the Spirit, you are not under the law.

Notice Paul contrasts the Spirit with both the flesh *and* the law. He later elaborates on this distinction in Romans 7–8. These mutually exclusive paths lead to different outcomes. The Spirit is in conflict with the flesh. What the apostle has in view here is not something as trivial as whether believers should or shouldn't perform particular rituals or actions. He's speaking more broadly of worldview and orientation. The Spirit and the law present radically different ways of living our lives.

Choosing to "gratify the desires of the flesh" (5:16) will ultimately cause us to veer off the road of faith in one of two directions. We may swerve to the left and find ourselves entangled in the lawlessness of pursuing "the lust of the flesh, the lust of the eyes, and the pride of life" (1 John 2:16). In this error, we replace God's will with our own. Alternately, we may veer to the right and stumble into the equally dangerous ditch of legalism, getting caught up in the thorny works of self-righteousness, moralizing, and boasting in our own efforts. In this error, we replace the gospel of Jesus with our own false gospel.

The same error—a focus on self, the pursuit of the gratification of our fleshly desires—can land us in either ditch. Jesus warned, "Small is the gate and narrow the road that leads to life, and only a few find it" (Matt. 7:14). We stay safely on the road by keeping our eyes not on ourselves but on Christ, who said, "My sheep listen to my voice; I know them, and they follow me" (John 10:27). He guides our steps, and He gets the glory.

If the Galatians allow the Judaizers to lead them into a self-focused way of life, they will end up in a ditch. "You who are trying to be justified by the law have . . . fallen away from grace" (5:4). Paul adds, "If you are led by the Spirit, you are not under the law" (5:18). It doesn't get much clearer than that. If we put ourselves under the law, we are not led by the Spirit because "the law is not based on faith" (3:12) but on doing. According to Paul, there is no such thing as a "Spirit-led law keeper." If we aren't being led by the Spirit, we will fall into works of the flesh:

> [19]The acts of the flesh are obvious: sexual immorality, impurity and debauchery; [20]idolatry and witchcraft; hatred, discord, jealousy, fits of rage, selfish ambition, dissensions, factions [21]and envy; drunkenness, orgies, and the like. I warn you, as I did before, that those who live like this will not inherit the kingdom of God.

We are not saved by our works, but what we do matters to God. Paul is not saying that if we fall into these fleshly acts, we can't repent and be forgiven or that our salvation hangs in the balance. Rather, he's speaking to "those who live like this" (5:21). The Greek verb *prassō* is a present tense, active participle. It describes an ongoing action: those who make a practice of doing these things. Paul is correcting the antinomian idea that living and continuing in these types of behavior is no big deal as long as we have faith. If this is how we are living our lives, we are not walking in the Spirit; we are still lost in our sin, and we'd better wake up and seek the true gospel.

Continuing with his "flesh versus Spirit" contrast, we now arrive at perhaps the most famous passage in Galatians. As opposed to the acts of the flesh, Paul describes what life looks like when we live in the freedom that Christ brought us and are led by the Holy Spirit:

> ²²But the fruit of the Spirit is love, joy, peace, forbearance, kindness, goodness, faithfulness, ²³gentleness and self-control. Against such things there is no law.

Notice Paul doesn't call it the "crown of the Spirit" to be placed on our heads for all the world to see. He calls it the *karpos*—the product or outcome—of the Spirit. And *karpos* is in the singular, meaning that this is not a list of various fruits for us to collect like merit badges. Rather, in the words of theologian Andrew Knowles, "It is the single fruit of a Christlike life."[9] And like the list of the acts of the flesh (5:19–21), this is a merely representative list. Paul paints a broad picture of each way of living to underscore the contrast.

Notably, all of the attributes of the fruit of the Spirit are legal; they conform with the old covenant law and God's OT expectations of His people. Believers in Jesus do not require the law to live godly lives; we are empowered by the Holy Spirit. At the same time, the Spirit will never lead us to break the principles of the law.

Jesus said, "I am the vine; you are the branches. If you remain in me and I in you, you will bear much fruit; apart from me you can do nothing" (John 15:5). As we abide in Christ, His Holy Spirit will produce in us, over time, good fruit. We cannot force these attributes into our lives through sheer willpower. And while they may not be immediately visible, they are the inevitable *karpos* of walking by the Spirit.

This fruit reflects God's character in a way that the law can't. Laws set limits, prohibit behavior, and prescribe activities. Conversely, this beautiful passage speaks in the language of grace. This is faith working in love, powered by the Holy Spirit. Its expression in our lives goes above and beyond what the law requires. When Christians walk by the Spirit and bear such fruit, there is no need for the law. This is the heart of Paul's pastoral counsel to the Galatians. He continues:

> 24Those who belong to Christ Jesus have crucified the flesh with its passions and desires. 25Since we live by the Spirit, let us keep in step with the Spirit. 26Let us not become conceited, provoking and envying each other.

Paul's admonition to "keep in step with the Spirit" (5:25) reveals that we have a role in walking out our faith. God could have set things up so that we instantly become morally perfect the moment we receive the Holy Spirit. But that is not how He chose to do it. This tells us something incredible about the living God. He prioritizes relationship over righteousness. Both matter, of course. But it is more important to God that we learn to depend on Him and walk with Him than become immediately sinless.

The Spirit-led process of sanctification is about becoming more Christlike and less sinful throughout our lives. It reveals that God isn't a cosmic policeman obsessed with us obeying all the rules. He's a loving, gracious Father who considers the gift and blessing of knowing Him more important than making us instantly sin-free.

If you think about it, moral imperfection in human beings isn't a challenge for God the way it is for us. He solved the problem of sin once and for all on the cross.[10] There is nothing more to be done. For those who have placed their faith in Christ, their ultimate moral perfection is a done deal (Rom. 8:30). And the more we learn to depend on Jesus and walk by His Spirit, the less we will sin as a natural consequence.

God's ultimate motive is love. The biggest blessing Yahweh can grant His beloved creatures is an active relationship with Him. The natural outworking of that relationship is moral righteousness, of course. But the *point* of it is love. When we come to faith in His Son, rather than saying, "You're all done, go have fun," God says, "You've just begun; keep in step with Me." He wants us to learn to lean on Him and depend on Him daily, even hourly, as we "keep in step with the Spirit" (5:25).

To extend Paul's metaphor, fruit grows best in fertile soil and a favorable climate. The soil for the fruit of the Spirit is a heart of faith, and the climate is one of prayer, worship, praise, reading God's Word, relationships with other believers, and serving those around us. The apostle isn't talking about the occasional influence of the Spirit. *Keeping in step* is a state of remaining in the Spirit. "No branch can bear fruit by itself; it must remain in the vine. Neither can you bear fruit unless you remain in me" (John 15:4).

Although Paul roundly rejects the idea that we are justified by keeping the law, he doesn't question the value of the law as a marker of God's will for us under the new covenant. In fact, he earlier told us how to fulfill the law: "The entire law is fulfilled in keeping this one command: 'Love your neighbor as yourself'" (5:14). If we live by the fruit of the Spirit, the law cannot condemn us (5:23).

Paul recognized that if the Galatians were to put themselves back under the obligation of the law, that would become the center of their Christian life, displacing the gospel of Jesus. This is exactly what was happening in the lives of the Judaizers. And it can just as easily happen to Christians today if we're not walking by the Spirit. Although morality matters to God, the ultimate Christian ideal, as taught by Jesus, isn't obedience to a moral code. It is abiding in Him (John 15:1–17). When that is our top priority, everything else falls into place. "Seek first his kingdom and his righteousness, and all these things will be given to you as well" (Matt. 6:33).

Notice Jesus didn't say, "Seek first *your own* righteousness." He is talking about a life in which, as theologian Wilfred Knox put it, "the Spirit of God is allowed to work freely and express itself in the spirit of man."[11] The famous author G. K. Chesterton saw it this way: "The more I considered Christianity, the more I found that while it had established a rule and order, the chief aim of that order was to give room for good things to run wild."[12] That is precisely the kind of freedom Paul preaches to his readers: the freedom for the good things of God to run wild in our lives. And now he turns to a practical application of what that looks like.

Galatians 5
Discussion Questions

1. Paul makes a big deal about the proper use of the Christian's freedom in Jesus. In what ways do you see the modern church affirming or compromising on that freedom?

2. Under the old covenant, circumcision was given as an identifying mark of God's people. What are some identifying "marks" of Christians under the new covenant? What signs or attributes do people of the world see in the life of a believer that tells them we belong to Christ?

3. What does it mean to "keep in step with the Spirit" (5:25)? What are some practical ways we can do this?

BEARING ONE ANOTHER'S BURDENS

Galatians 6:1–10

❧

Conflict is unavoidable in apologetics. Opposing false teachings necessarily requires confrontation. But this should never be a case of arguing for the sake of arguing. Apologetics is not about winning arguments, scoring points, or proving the other guy wrong; it's about saving souls. It's about defending what is true and pointing to the gospel of Jesus. With everything he has stirred up in this letter, Paul, the concerned pastor, understands that his *apologia* must be accompanied by a call for love and unity in the church:

> ¹Brothers and sisters, if someone is caught in a sin, you who live by the Spirit should restore that person gently. But watch yourselves, or you also may be tempted. ²Carry each other's burdens, and in this way you will fulfill the law of Christ. ³If anyone thinks they are something when they are not, they deceive themselves. ⁴Each one should test their own actions. Then they can take pride in themselves alone, without comparing themselves to someone else, ⁵for each one should carry their

> own load. [6]Nevertheless, the one who receives instruction in
> the word should share all good things with their instructor.

The practical side of loving one another and living in humility under the guidance of the Holy Spirit is bearing one another's burdens. Paul begins by showing how sin should be addressed in a community of believers: "If someone is caught in a sin . . ." (6:1). He could be speaking of being caught doing something wrong or, more broadly, being trapped in sin. Either way, the apostle does not advise the Galatians to kick wayward believers out of their community as he does with the Judaizers who were openly teaching a false gospel.

Sadly, banishing fallen believers often happens too quickly in the modern church. One pastor I spoke with lamented that the church can be too quick to "shoot the wounded." When we see an influential Christian fall from grace, ensnared in sin, we tend to stand on the outside and point our fingers. Paul warns against such an approach. Rather, "Restore that person gently" (6:1). Put your arm around your fallen brother or sister, show them mercy, and help them repent, repair, and rebuild.

Notice that these are instructions for approaching a fellow believer in the context of a faith community. This is not how we are to approach unbelievers who have been overtaken by sin. If individuals have not yet placed themselves under the lordship of Jesus, that is an entirely different conversation. Author Christopher Cone writes, "For those who have not believed in the Person of Jesus the Christ there is really only one ethical mandate: *to believe in Him.*"[1] "Without faith it is impossible to please God" (Heb. 11:6). Paul's pastoral counsel in Galatians 6 is for the family of believers.

If brothers or sisters have been overtaken by sin, the burden of responsibility for helping them falls on "you who live by the Spirit" (6:1). Paul is speaking of those who "keep in step with the Spirit" (5:25) and are bearing fruit (5:22–23). And what should they do? "*Restore* that person" (6:1, emphasis added). The Greek verb is *katartizo*, which means "restore to its former condition." It is the same word used in the Gospels to refer to the mending of fishing nets (Matt. 4:21). *Katartizo* means we do the hard work of rolling up our sleeves, walking alongside our brother or sister in Christ, and helping them.

This passage tells us two things about how we should restore errant fellow believers. The first has to do with love. In Galatians 2, we saw that Peter separated himself from the Gentiles "because he was afraid of those who belonged to the circumcision group" (2:12). They were intimidating him. By contrast, we should restore our fellow believers "in a spirit of gentleness" (6:1 ESV). And gentleness, by the way, is a fruit of the Spirit (5:23). Don't rub their nose in it; don't strong-arm them like the Judaizers were doing. The apostle's second directive is to "watch yourselves, or you also may be tempted" (6:1). Be alert and careful so you don't fall into sin along with them. No one is above temptation.

Paul goes on to say, "Carry each other's burdens, and in this way you will fulfill the law of Christ" (6:2). Here is another interesting turn of phrase: "the law of Christ." It is only found in one other place in the Bible. In 1 Corinthians, Paul uses "law of Christ" to distinguish a Christian's obligations from those of the old covenant law:

> To the Jews I became like a Jew, to win the Jews. To those under the law I became like one under the law (though I myself am not under the law), so as to win those under the law. To those not having the law I became like one not having the law (though I am not free from God's law but am under Christ's law), so as to win those not having the law. (1 Cor. 9:20–21)

Paul declares, "I myself am not under the law" (v. 20) . . . "but am under Christ's law" (v. 21). He draws a distinction between the law of Moses and the law of Christ. The same is true of all

Christians. We are under the "law of Christ." Of course, Jesus did not give a formal "law" as Yahweh did with the Israelites in thunder and lightning at Mount Sinai. However, He did issue His own commandments and moral principles from atop a different mountain. On the northwestern shore of the Sea of Galilee, near Capernaum, He climbed the Mount of Beatitudes and sat down to teach what we have come to call the Sermon on the Mount (Matt. 5–7).

In Galatians 6, when Paul writes, "fulfill the law of Christ" (6:2), he is not using legal language. Rather, the Greek word *nomos* is used in the sense of a principle or norm. To fulfill the *nomos of Christ*—we might even call it the *Torah of Messiah*—means to live the way Jesus taught us to live. We satisfy the direction and instruction of Jesus by loving and helping others and bearing each other's burdens (6:2). This is the heart of Christ:

> A new command I give you: Love one another. As I have loved you, so you must love one another. (John 13:34)

> Greater love has no one than this: to lay down one's life for one's friends. (John 15:13)

> Even the Son of Man did not come to be served, but to serve, and to give his life as a ransom for many. (Mark 10:45)

The *law* of Christ is the *way* of Christ. Everything He taught was grounded in the two greatest commandments: love God and love others (Matt. 22:36–40). This is precisely what Paul tells the Galatians: "The entire law is fulfilled in keeping this one command: 'Love your neighbor as yourself'" (5:14). He repeats the same thing in Romans: "Whoever loves others has fulfilled the law" (Rom. 13:8). Everything the law demands is fulfilled when we love others with a genuine, biblical love. That is what obedience to Jesus looks like.

In Galatians 6, Paul goes on to say, "If anyone thinks they are something when they are not, they deceive themselves" (6:3). To love and gentleness, he adds humility. Don't correct fellow believers in a spirit of pride and arrogance, thinking that you are better than them. It could just as easily be you who gets caught in sin. The apostle may be anticipating a caustic, un-Christlike response to his letter in which some Galatians begin persecuting their fellow believers who were lured into the Judaizers' false theology. He encourages them to gently and humbly *katartizo* (restore) their fallen brothers and sisters to the true gospel beliefs they held before the false teachers got a hold of them.

Paul goes on to say:

> Each one should test their own actions. Then they can take pride
> in themselves alone, without comparing themselves to someone
> else, for each one should carry their own load. (6:4–5)

This is both wise counsel and a jab at the Judaizers. Paul has already accused them of making much of themselves (4:17). Inherent in legalism is the sinful tendency to compare ourselves to others. The apostle has already warned about this: "If you bite and devour each other, watch out or you will be destroyed by each other" (5:15). His list of works of the flesh in the last chapter includes "discord," "jealousy," "selfish ambition," and "factions" (5:20). The law of Christ, on the other hand, would not have us exploit the failures or weaknesses of others. Instead, it leads us to restore them gently.

Paul tells the Galatians, *Keep your eyes on your own paper. Don't compare yourself to your neighbor like the Judaizers are doing.* Jesus put it this way: "First take the plank out of your own eye, and then you will see clearly to remove the speck from your brother's eye" (Matt. 7:5). The psalmist wrote:

> Search me, God, and know my heart;
> test me and know my anxious thoughts.

> See if there is any offensive way in me,
>> and lead me in the way everlasting. (Ps. 139:23–24)

When Paul says, "Each one should carry their own load" (6:5), he is speaking of a sober, Spirit-led self-examination of our hearts. We're each individually responsible to God for how we live out our faith. We won't be judged for how others did or how others think we did.

At first glance, it might seem that Paul contradicts himself. He says, "Carry each other's burdens" (6:2) and "Each one should carry their own load" (6:5). There are two different Greek words at play. In Galatians 6:2, Paul uses *barose*, meaning "a heavy or weighty burden." Three verses later, he uses *phortion*, which carries the idea of a backpack or a soldier's pack. The law of Christ commands us to help each other bear the heavy burdens of life (6:2). This is why community and fellowship are so important. However, there are also personal spiritual responsibilities that we each need to bear for ourselves (6:4–5).

Paul adds another responsibility: "The one who receives instruction in the word should share all good things with their instructor" (6:6). The idea of sharing "all good things" is primarily a reference to physical resources. The apostle provides a real-world example of how the believers in Galatia can bear one another's burdens. Teachers of God's Word share their spiritual gifts with other believers, so those believers should share their financial gifts with their teachers. You have to wonder if this encouragement stems from the Galatians' clear need for sound biblical guidance in light of the present controversy with the Judaizers.

To illustrate his point, Paul invokes the agricultural principle of sowing and reaping:

> 7Do not be deceived: God cannot be mocked. A man reaps what he sows. 8Whoever sows to please their flesh, from the

> flesh will reap destruction; whoever sows to please the Spirit, from the Spirit will reap eternal life. [9]Let us not become weary in doing good, for at the proper time we will reap a harvest if we do not give up. [10]Therefore, as we have opportunity, let us do good to all people, especially to those who belong to the family of believers.

Paul picks up a theme he has touched on several times in this letter: the contrast between flesh and spirit. Here, that distinction is framed in the context of sowing and reaping to explain why we should bear each other's burdens gently and humbly. Because we all reap what we sow, it's important to sow in the right places and in the right way.

"Do not be deceived: God cannot be mocked. A man reaps what he sows" (6:7). The law of sowing and reaping was established by God, so don't mock Him by thinking you're exempt from it. In bringing up this subject on the heels of urging the Galatians to support their spiritual teachers, Paul links the two ideas:

Whoever sows to please their flesh, from the flesh will reap destruction; whoever sows to please the Spirit, from the Spirit will reap eternal life. (6:8)

This passage speaks to doctrines like "works-righteousness" and eternal security ("once saved, always saved") and has been the source of sketchy theological ideas. "Works-righteousness" folks like the Judaizers often read this passage as teaching that believers save themselves by their good works. They interpret Paul as teaching that we will lose our salvation if we do not do the "work" of sowing to the Spirit.

However, the apostle is not only contrasting destruction and eternal life but also talking about the place from which one will reap their harvest: "Whoever sows to please their flesh, *from the flesh* will reap destruction" (6:8, emphasis added). The flesh is the source of the corruption. Conversely, "Whoever sows to please the Spirit, *from the Spirit* will reap eternal life" (6:8, emphasis added). Salvation comes from the Spirit, not from the flesh or our works. Paul's metaphor has two layers of meaning: a direct application and a broader principle. And in neither case is he teaching that it's up to us to secure our own salvation by doing good works. (If Paul teaches "salvation by faith plus works" here, he's contradicting everything else he wrote in this letter!)

As for the direct application, consider the immediate context. In the opening verses of Galatians 6, Paul encourages believers to support one another. He then applies this idea to teachers (6:6) and invokes the law of sowing and reaping (6:7–8). Seen in that light, the concept of sowing to the flesh is about spending our money and resources on "works of the flesh," such as sexual immorality, impurity, rivalries, and drunkenness (5:19–21). If we invest our time and resources into these works of the flesh, we will reap a harvest of remorse and shame. After all, the flesh ultimately dies and decays. Jesus taught:

> Do not store up for yourselves treasures on earth, where moths and vermin destroy, and where thieves break in and steal. But store up for yourselves treasures in heaven, where moths and vermin do not destroy, and where thieves do not break in and steal. For where your treasure is, there your heart will be also. . . . You cannot serve both God and money. (Matt. 6:19–21, 24)

How we spend our money and resources reveals the true motivations of our hearts. Paul warns that Christians who invest in the gratification of their flesh are insulting God. "Sowing to the flesh" reveals that our hearts are in the wrong place, and the seeds we sow into our flesh will amount to nothing in the end. Conversely, "whoever sows to please the Spirit, from the Spirit will reap eternal life" (6:8). The believer who invests in the Lord's work—which in the immediate context is linked to supporting spiritual teachers and investing in ministry work—will reap a harvest that will last forever. Souls will be saved for all eternity.

There are two ways in which the Greek phrase *aiōnios zōē* (eternal life) is used in Scripture. Most commonly, it describes the never-ending life that believers receive at the end of their earthly lives. But it's also applied to the new life we are given at the moment we are reborn. Jesus said, "Whoever believes in the Son *has* (present tense) eternal life" (John 3:36, emphasis added). Paul writes elsewhere, "Therefore, if anyone *is* (present tense) in Christ, he is a new creation. The old has passed away; behold, the new has come" (2 Cor. 5:17 ESV, emphasis added). Our eternal life begins the moment we place our faith in Jesus.

When Paul speaks of sowing and reaping in Galatians 6, he's also saying that those who sow to the things of the Spirit will reap benefits *in this life* that those who sow to the flesh will not. And we will all ultimately have to account for how we live our lives. Paul writes elsewhere:

> So we make it our goal to please him . . . For we must all appear before the judgment seat of Christ, so that each of us may receive what is due us for the things done while in the body, whether good or bad. (2 Cor. 5:9–10)

The broader application of Paul's sowing and reaping metaphor applies to all Christians. He isn't describing the process of God stepping in to render judgment; He already rendered His judgment when we were justified by faith in Christ. Rather, "sowing and reaping" is about the long-term natural consequences of our actions in God's universe. In the same way that continually bingeing on junk food puts us on a crash course for a health crisis later in life, repeatedly "sowing to the flesh" puts us on a crash course for a spiritual crisis. If we persistently follow our sinful nature, we will reap spiritual collapse and destruction. There are still natural consequences for sin in the life of a believer. We all know that sin can be fun in the moment. But it never yields a harvest of joy, peace, and life.

We also need to read Paul's warning in light of the rest of his letter to the Galatians. He means something particular when he speaks of sowing to please the sinful nature. Our sinful nature is the part of us that resists the free grace of the gospel. It's the part of us that is susceptible to the works-based false gospel of the Judaizers. It deceives us into trying to accomplish in the flesh what can only be completed by the Spirit. Our sinful nature wants us to get some of the glory when all glory rightfully belongs to God alone. "For the desires of the flesh are against the Spirit, and the desires of the Spirit are against the flesh, for these are opposed to each other" (5:17 ESV). Paul shows us how our sinful nature can lead us to fall back into some degree of slavery to sin, even though we have already been set free. It's as if part of us wants to put the shackles back on our wrists. And when believers are in this state of mind, we can lose sight of the gospel.

This is part of the Spirit-led sanctification process. Everyone's journey is different because every human being is different. We don't all mature in our likeness to Christ in a nice straight line. But as we walk out our sanctification, the fact never changes that we have already been justified. Just because we stumble or lose sight of the truth for a time or go through a period of discipline from God does not mean that we stop being saved by God's grace. After all, He sent the people of Israel into exile and scattered them across the nations, but He never stopped loving them. His promise that a remnant of Israel will be saved still remains. Likewise, if our faith is genuine, our salvation is secure too.

Some in the early Christian communities participated in church gatherings and did good works but had not actually placed their faith in Jesus. Some were still on the journey. Others were outright acting hypocritically, and their hearts were far from God. The latter seems to be Paul's view of the Judaizers in Galatia because of the false gospel they preached. In this passage about sowing and reaping, Paul also warns that if we persist in putting ourselves under the old covenant law and working for our own righteousness, we are rejecting Jesus and everything He did for us. As he cautioned earlier, "If you let yourselves be circumcised, Christ will be of no value to you at all" (5:2).

Believers who find themselves wandering away from the gospel and trying to earn God's approval through good works will inevitably experience a loss of peace, joy, and fruitfulness in their lives for a time. And if they persist and come to officially embrace the belief that their righteousness can (or should) be earned by their works, they are turning their back on Jesus and serving a false gospel.

Consider the contrasts Paul has used in comparing the flesh and the Spirit. He asked the Galatians, "After beginning by means of the Spirit, are you now trying to finish by means of the flesh?" (3:3). In the allegory of Isaac and Ishmael, he said, "At that time the son born according to the flesh persecuted the son born by the power of the Spirit. It is the same now" (4:29). In chapter 5, he said: "For the flesh desires what is contrary to the Spirit, and the Spirit what is contrary to the flesh" (5:17). Here in Galatians 6, Paul sharply draws that contrast yet again: "Whoever sows to please their flesh, from the flesh will reap destruction; whoever sows to please the Spirit, from the Spirit will reap eternal life" (6:8).

These are mutually exclusive ways of living our lives. The apostle accordingly encourages his readers to continue to walk in the Spirit and fulfill the law of Christ: "Let us not become weary in doing good, for at the proper time we will reap a harvest if we do not give up" (6:9). He isn't saying that if we grow weary of doing good, we won't make it to heaven. Rather, he uses the sowing and reaping metaphor to remind us that we are playing the long game. Paul is encouraging the Galatians—and, by extension, believers today—to take heart, because the law of sowing and reaping *will* yield its reward in due season.

In the literal sense of sowing and reaping, a farmer doesn't reap a harvest until long after the seeds are sown. Similarly, Paul says, *Trust the process, keep sowing into spiritual things. Keep supporting your teachers and ministries that are devoted to the Word of God, and you will reap a reward.* He stirs up his readers to finish strong because he knows from personal experience that just as the life of Jesus was marked by suffering, so, too, are the lives of His followers.

For Christians, suffering is part of the sanctification process. Following Jesus is not for the fainthearted. He told us as much: "Whoever wants to be my disciple must deny themselves and take up their cross and follow me" (Matt. 16:24). Paul elsewhere teaches that believers are "heirs of God and co-heirs with Christ, if indeed we share in his sufferings in order that we may also share in his glory" (Rom. 8:17). This is what the famous German theologian Dietrich Bonhoeffer called "the cost of discipleship."[2] It is the willingness to give up everything for Christ.

Despite what the prosperity gospel promises, believers don't get to "name and claim" health and wealth in the name of Jesus. We can't use the "power of faith" to create our own reality and get what we want, as the Word of Faith movement teaches. These are not biblical concepts. They are a Christianized version of the pagan, new age notion of *manifesting*, which claims we can create our own reality through positive thinking. The Bible teaches nothing of the sort. Don't misunderstand; faith, healing, and blessings are all biblical realities. But they are given by God for *His* glory, not ours. The living God is not a genie in a bottle; He is our holy and sovereign Lord.

Self-help preachers want to teach us how to have our best life now, but the Bible says suffering is a part of following Christ. We don't seek out suffering for its own sake, of course. It is part and parcel of following Jesus in a fallen world. Christian suffering can certainly come in the form of persecution, imprisonment, and even martyrdom. But for most believers, especially those in Western cultures, suffering for Christ looks like serving others rather than pampering ourselves; denying our fleshly desires for sex, wealth, and glory; sacrificing our hard-earned money and resources to bless others; or being misunderstood and socially ostracized for our loyalty to the word of God. This is part of our sanctification process; it tests and refines our faith. "We also glory in our sufferings, because we know that suffering produces perseverance; perseverance, character; and character, hope" (Rom. 5:3–4). Paul, of all people, knows this.[3] In light of this reality, he encourages his readers: "Let us not become weary in doing good" (6:9). It's going to be tough, but in due season we will reap a harvest.

Paul adds, "Therefore, as we have opportunity, let us do good to all people, especially to those who belong to the family of believers" (6:10). This is the biblical role of works in the life of a Christian. Our good works flow from placing our faith and trust in Jesus. We are to "do good to all people," especially fellow believers. This statement also includes our enemies and those who persecute us (Matt. 5:43–44). Followers of Jesus are called to "overcome evil with good" (Rom. 12:21).[4] Such good works are part of our suffering and sacrifice as Christians. The author of Hebrews urges, "Do not forget to do good and to share with others, for with such sacrifices God is pleased" (Heb. 13:16). When we "walk by the Spirit" (5:16), our lives begin to show the fruit of the Spirit (5:22–23). Paul now closes his letter with a final warning and a benediction.

A FINAL WARNING & BENEDICTION

Galatians 6:11–18

In antiquity, letters were often dictated to an *amanuensis* (scribe). For example, Jeremiah dictated his words to Baruch (Jer. 36:4) and Isaiah had disciples who recorded his words (Isa. 8:16). The apostle Paul did the same thing, and would often add a farewell message in his own handwriting.[1] For example, at the end of 2 Thessalonians, he says, "I, Paul, write this greeting in my own hand, which is the distinguishing mark in all my letters. This is how I write" (2 Thess. 3:17). He then adds a final sentence: "The grace of our Lord Jesus Christ be with you all" (2 Thess. 3:18). The apostle takes a similar, though more impassioned, approach in Galatians:

> ¹¹See what large letters I use as I write to you with my own hand!

We can make two interesting observations about this verse. First, scholars are divided on whether it indicates that Paul wrote the entire letter in his own hand or just the farewell section.

(Particularly since the epistle doesn't mention an amanuensis like some of his other letters do.) Second, *why* did the apostle write in large letters? Scholars suggest he may have written in *uncial* letters (large, block script) due to a problem with his eyesight or because he had poor Greek handwriting.[2] However, neither issue is mentioned anywhere in Scripture.

Since this is the only letter in which Paul highlights his large handwriting, and because we've seen how passionate he is about guarding his beloved Galatians against false teachings, I believe he used large letters for emphasis. He summons up all of his apostolic authority as he now brings the conversation back to the Judaizers. We saw earlier that the opening salutation of Galatians does not follow Paul's typical pattern, and neither does this farewell section. He ordinarily signs off with just a line or two. However, at the end of Galatians, compelled by concern and righteous anger, Paul pens a farewell paragraph:

> [12]Those who want to impress people by means of the flesh are trying to compel you to be circumcised. The only reason they do this is to avoid being persecuted for the cross of Christ. [13]Not even those who are circumcised keep the law, yet they want you to be circumcised that they may boast about your circumcision in the flesh. [14]May I never boast except in the cross of our Lord Jesus Christ, through which the world has been crucified to me, and I to the world. [15]Neither circumcision nor uncircumcision means anything; what counts is the new creation.

The motivation for the Judaizers is twofold. First, they are eager to escape harassment as professing Christians: "The only reason they do this is to avoid being persecuted for the cross of Christ" (6:12).

This could refer to the political persecution that many first-century believers experienced as a result of confessing faith in Jesus. At that time the Roman Empire recognized Judaism as an approved faith, but Christianity was *religio illicita* (an illegal religion). The Judaizers may have been publicly promoting the practice of circumcision so they could be seen as Jews, not Christians. It's also possible they were concerned about their reputation as law keepers among their Jewish friends and family and wanted to avoid the social persecution that came with professing faith in Christ alone.

Second, the Judaizers want to brag about their converts: "They want you to be circumcised that they may boast about your circumcision in the flesh" (6:13). The false teachers revel in the praise of men rather than God: "What they want is to alienate you from us, so that you may have zeal for them" (4:17). Their primary goal—like many heretical movements today—wasn't to lead lost people to Christ or help fellow believers grow in grace. Rather, their chief aim was to win more converts to their own agenda so they could brag about it.

Paul adds, "Not even those who are circumcised keep the law" (6:13). There are a couple ways we might take this statement. Robert Jamieson suggests that the Judaizers had arbitrarily selected circumcision out of the whole law, as if that one thing was enough to cover their non-observance of the rest of the law.[3] That may be part of it. Paul also seems to be saying that circumcision alone does not elevate anyone to the level of a law keeper. He said earlier that every man who accepts circumcision is obligated to keep the whole law (5:3). In other words (pardon the pun), circumcision alone does not cut it.

The Judaizers may have belonged to the same party of Pharisees about whom Jesus said, "They do not practice what they preach" (Matt. 23:3). Paul targets the hypocrisy of the false teachers, showing that their veneration of the law was a ruse. Their real motivation was winning converts to their cause; this made them feel good about themselves and look righteous to others. But the only appropriate source of our boasting is the cross of Christ:

> ¹⁴May I never boast except in the cross of our Lord Jesus Christ, through which the world has been crucified to me, and I to the world. ¹⁵Neither circumcision nor uncircumcision means anything; what counts is the new creation.

The Judaizers were concentrating their attention on what theologians call *adiaphora*: matters of indifference. Under Jesus and the new covenant, it does not matter whether we are circumcised. Elsewhere, Paul writes:

> Was a man already circumcised when he was called? He should not become uncircumcised. Was a man uncircumcised when he was called? He should not be circumcised. Circumcision is nothing and uncircumcision is nothing. Keeping God's commands is what counts. Each person should remain in the situation they were in when God called them. (1 Cor. 7:18–20)

Circumcision was a visible marker given under the old covenant to indicate that Israel belonged to Yahweh. By contrast, when we are in Christ, "neither circumcision nor uncircumcision has any value. The only thing that counts is faith expressing itself through love" (5:6). God's requirement for this distinction in the flesh came to an end: "There is neither Jew nor Gentile . . . for you are all one in Christ Jesus" (3:28). Therefore, "Neither circumcision nor uncircumcision means anything; what counts is the new creation" (6:15). And "if anyone is in Christ, the new creation has come" (2 Cor. 5:17).

Paul continues:

> ¹⁶Peace and mercy to all who follow this rule—to the Israel of God.

By "this rule," the apostle refers to his declaration that it's not works of the law that count, but "the new creation" (6:15). He is speaking of the rule of being led by the Spirit, not by the flesh; of being justified by faith in Christ, not by works of the law; of not boasting in our flesh but in the cross of Jesus; and of choosing freedom in Christ over slavery to the law. Paul wishes "peace and mercy to all who follow this rule" (6:16), whom he then refers to as "the Israel of God."

This is the only place in the Bible that phrase is found, and the way this sentence is worded in Greek is interesting. The NIV translates the text as: "Peace and mercy to all who follow this rule—to the Israel of God," which leaves out a small but important Greek word. Where the NIV puts a dash, the Greek text uses the conjunction *kai* ("and, also"). So, the text would be more literally translated as ". . . to all who follow this rule and (*kai*) to the Israel of God."[4] What's going on here?

Grammatically, the Greek could be interpreted a couple of ways, depending on how we apply the conjunction *kai*. The statement "Peace and mercy to all who follow this rule *and* to the Israel of God" could refer to two distinct groups. Paul could be wishing peace and mercy on: (1) Those who walk by this rule and (2) Jewish believers in Jesus. However, this interpretation creates an arbitrary distinction that leads to a "two law" theology in which Jewish believers apparently do not follow the same rules that other believers do. And yet Paul expressly declared earlier, "There is neither Jew nor Gentile . . . you are all one in Christ Jesus" (3:28).

I believe this verse is better understood as Paul saying that "all who follow this rule" *are* the Israel of God. This is likely why the NIV rendered the text the way it did. Paul wishes peace and mercy on those who believe in salvation by grace through faith in Christ as individual believers *and* as the collective family or "Israel" of God. He wrote earlier: "If you belong to Christ, then you are Abraham's seed, and heirs according to the promise" (3:29). It is no longer about genealogy but faith. The "Israel of God" refers to the church, the body of Christ comprised of both Jewish and Gentile believers.

Paul fills out this idea in his letter to the Romans:

It is not as though God's word had failed. For not all who are descended from Israel are Israel. Nor because they are his descendants are they all Abraham's children. On the contrary, "It is through Isaac that your offspring will be reckoned." In other words, it is not the children by physical descent who are God's children, but it is the children of the promise who are regarded as Abraham's offspring. (Rom. 9:6–8)

This idea would have particularly stung the Jewish Judaizers. It was as offensive to them as Paul's teaching about the true seed of Abraham in Galatians 3 and his allegory of Sarah and Hagar in Galatians 4. The false teachers in Galatia were trying to bring believers in Jesus back under the OT law, which Paul equates to slavery at least eight times in this letter.[5] Yet those who believe in Christ are the true "Israel of God," Abraham's children through faith in Jesus, not through the flesh.

At this point, a word of caution is in order. Over the centuries, some Christians have used Paul's phrase as the basis for an unbiblical theology called *supersessionism*, or "replacement theology," which teaches that the church has replaced Israel in God's sovereign plans. They believe that God no longer has a specific future plan for Israel or the Jews. The Bible teaches otherwise. Paul writes about the future salvation of Israel in Romans 11:25–32. The church has not replaced Israel in God's grand story of redemption. The old family has not been cast out and supplanted. Instead, the definition of God's household has been expanded to include all people who have placed their faith in His Son, Jesus, whether they are Jew or Gentile, man or woman, slave or free. If we have faith in Jesus, we have been adopted into God's family (4:5); we are offspring of Abraham (3:29), the Israel of God (6:16).

Paul closes his epistle with these words:

> [17]From now on, let no one cause me trouble, for I bear on my body the marks of Jesus.
>
> [18]The grace of our Lord Jesus Christ be with your spirit, brothers and sisters. Amen.

There is a sense of exasperation in the way the letter ends. It's as if Paul is saying, *I have faithfully taught and suffered for the true gospel and have scars on my body to prove it; I should have earned your trust and respect by now.* Nevertheless, it is notable that he began this letter with a blessing of grace to his readers (1:3) and closes it the same way (6:18). Paul has educated his beloved Galatians as a church historian and theological professor. He has expressed concern for them as a pastor and spiritual mentor. Despite mounting a passionate, strongly worded argument that included many warnings and reprimands, he still ends with affection, referring to his readers as *adelphoi*, brothers and sisters.

Galatians 6
Discussion Questions

1. Have you ever been involved in restoring brothers or sisters in Christ who were caught up in sin or a false belief system? What are some ways to approach them and offer help? What are the dangers in doing so?

2. Paul says we fulfill the law of Christ by bearing one another's burdens (6:2). Do you think he is teaching that loving and serving one another is just for fellow believers? Or does it extend beyond the walls of the church to the people in our community, including unbelievers?

3. Paul says, "God is not mocked" regarding the law of sowing and reaping (6:7 ESV). What is the difference between questioning God's commands in a mocking or rebellious way and wrestling with them sincerely and honestly?

CONCLUSION

In the warm, dusty room where the Galatians had gathered to hear Paul's letter, his closing words echoed in their ears:

> From now on, let no one cause me trouble, for I bear on my body the marks of Jesus.
>
> The grace of our Lord Jesus Christ be with your spirit, brothers and sisters. Amen. (6:17–18)

Perhaps they sat in silence for a long moment, their minds reeling. Their spiritual mentor had taken them on a turbulent journey. Surely, they would want to read through his letter again. The one big inescapable idea that the apostle hammered home repeatedly—the thesis statement that Professor Paul proved and defended from every angle—is that we are made right with God through faith in Jesus, not by works of the law.

This was why Paul wrote of meeting the other apostles in Jerusalem where "not even Titus, who was with me, was compelled to be circumcised" (2:3). As Paul defiantly proclaimed concerning the false teachers, "We did not give in to them for a moment, so that the truth of the gospel might be preserved for you" (2:5). It's also why the apostle recounted his public rebuke of Peter, concluding, "So we, too, have put our faith in Christ Jesus that we may be justified by faith in Christ and not by the works of the law" (2:16).

Paul invoked the faith of the patriarch Abraham to further bolster his thesis, showing how Jesus fulfilled God's promise:

> Christ redeemed us from the curse of the law by becoming a curse for us . . . in order that the blessing given to Abraham might come to the Gentiles through Christ Jesus, so that by faith we might receive the promise of the Spirit. (3:13, 14)

The apostle argued, "If a law had been given that could impart life, then righteousness would certainly have come by the law" (3:21), but that's not how God did it. Instead, "the law was our guardian until Christ came that we might be justified by faith. Now that this faith has come, we are no longer under a guardian" (3:24–25). God sent His Son "to redeem those under the law, that we might receive adoption to sonship" (4:5).

Paul then developed the idea of sonship in his allegory of Sarah and Hagar, demonstrating that the old covenant law "bears children who are to be slaves" (4:24), yet those who trust in Christ "are not children of the slave woman, but of the free woman" (4:31). With respect to the law, Paul concludes, "It is for freedom that Christ has set us free. Stand firm, then, and do not let yourselves be burdened again by a yoke of slavery" (5:1). He further showed that the ritual of circumcision, which was a commandment under the old covenant, no longer has any value or meaning. Rather, in Christ Jesus, what counts is "faith expressing itself through love" (5:6) and the new creation we become in Him (6:15).

The reading of a letter in the first century was commonly followed by a time of discussion and interpretation of the message. Wouldn't you love to have been a fly on the wall during that conversation? How were the Judaizers treated? Had Paul's letter changed anyone's mind? How did the Jewish believers feel about sharing their inheritance with Gentiles? How did the Gentiles feel about becoming children of the God of Israel? Unfortunately, history is silent on that discussion. But we know that this epistle has had a significant impact on the church throughout history. It has also had a tremendous influence on the discipline of apologetics.

One thing I have learned by regularly engaging with modern-day Judaizers is that one rarely arrives at false beliefs through a purely logical process of deduction. Rather, false theologies are formed through a complex blend of emotional investment, theological misunderstanding, spiritual deception, and personal identity. Once we've committed to and publicly proclaimed an errant idea, it can be difficult and painful to admit our mistake and repent. As C. S. Lewis observed, "We all want progress . . . [but] if you are on the wrong road, progress means doing an about-turn and walking back to the right road."[1] It can take some time to admit (to ourselves and others) that we are on the wrong road.

When it comes to the Galatians dealing with the Judaizers among them—or modern Christians faced with false teachers—this epistle has much to teach us. Paul did not simply claim the Judaizers were wrong. He took the time to build a logical case based on biblical evidence and appealed to reason and fact. He also warned the Galatians to remove the bad yeast and cast out the Judaizers using strong, passionate language: "As for those agitators, I wish they would go the whole way and emasculate themselves!" (5:12). This was appropriate for the situation at hand. However, Paul did not always use such dramatic, confrontational tactics. For example, in his approach with the Athenian philosophers he instead spoke respectfully and sought common ground: "I see that in every way you are very religious" (Acts 17:22). Paul's harshest rebukes were saved for those who knew better.

The apostle Peter likewise adjusted his tone to fit his audience. When writing to believers who were discouraged by the persecution they were encountering, he taught a gentle approach:

> Always be prepared to give an answer to everyone who asks you to give the reason for the hope that you have. But do this with gentleness and respect, keeping a clear conscience, so that those who speak maliciously against your good behavior in Christ may be ashamed of their slander. (1 Peter 3:15–16)

Conversely, when writing of false teachers who ought to know better, Peter pulled no punches:

> These people are springs without water and mists driven by a storm. Blackest darkness is reserved for them. For they mouth empty, boastful words and, by appealing to the lustful desires of the flesh, they entice people who are just escaping from those who live in error . . . If they have escaped the corruption of the world by knowing our Lord and Savior Jesus Christ and are again entangled in it and are overcome, they are worse off at the end than they were at the beginning . . . Of them the proverbs are true: "A dog returns to its vomit," and, "A sow that is washed returns to her wallowing in the mud." (2 Peter 2:17–18, 20, 22)

Paul and Peter learned to vary their tone from Jesus. With the Pharisees and religious leaders, His rebukes were harsh and filled with righteous anger:

> Woe to you, teachers of the law and Pharisees, you hypocrites! You travel over land and sea to win a single convert, and when you have succeeded, you make them twice as much a child of hell as you are. (Matt. 23:15)[2]

On the other hand, Jesus was gentle with the public and believers who wanted to learn, like the disciples:

An argument started among the disciples as to which of them would be the greatest. Jesus, knowing their thoughts, took a little child and had him stand beside him. Then he said to them, "Whoever welcomes this little child in my name welcomes me; and whoever welcomes me welcomes the one who sent me. For it is the one who is least among you all who is the greatest." (Luke 9:46–48)

Prayerful discernment is a requirement for any Christian addressing false teachings. There is a necessary difference in how we approach a wayward believer and how we confront a false teacher who is influencing others. Jesus reserved His harshest words for teachers in a position of influence who were leading others astray. His brother James warned, "Not many of you should become teachers, my fellow believers, because you know that we who teach will be judged more strictly" (James 3:1).

That said, the principle behind both approaches is the same. The church is expected to confront false teachings and counterfeit gospels. This can be a tall order in our current cultural climate, where disagreement is often mislabeled "hatred" or "intolerance." Not every Christian is called or even expected to be a trained apologist, of course. But we are commanded to "always be prepared to give an answer to everyone who asks you to give the reason for the hope that you have" (1 Peter 3:15). As the body of Christ, we should not tolerate any doctrine that threatens the gospel of Jesus. To do so would be to let a little bad yeast ruin the loaf (Gal. 5:9).

Here's the catch. In order to recognize false teachings, we need to first be familiar with what the Bible actually says. Paul's arguments in Galatians highlight why biblical literacy is so important. The more time we spend reading and studying the Word, the better we understand the true gospel and the quicker we will recognize a counterfeit. This doesn't necessarily mean that all Christians will agree on every issue. There are many secondary and tertiary issues on which honest believers can differ. Paul calls these "disputable matters" (Rom. 14:1) and urges believers to "stop passing judgment on one another" (Rom. 14:13) on such issues. But any teaching that threatens the essence of the gospel or the sufficiency of Christ must be dealt with directly, prayerfully, and scripturally. I pray that our journey through Galatians has been helpful in that regard.

> For though we live in the world, we do not wage war as the world does. The weapons we fight with are not the weapons of the world. On the contrary, they have divine power to demolish strongholds. We demolish arguments and every pretension that sets itself up against the knowledge of God, and we take captive every thought to make it obedient to Christ. (2 Cor. 10:3–5)

ACKNOWLEDGMENTS

As a professor, I approach my YouTube channel *Defending the Biblical Roots of Christianity* as a laboratory of sorts. It's not only an online "classroom" for teachings and Bible studies but also an arena in which I try to spark conversation, challenge conventions, and get people thinking. This book began as a video series on that channel, and I owe a debt of gratitude to all our viewers who weighed in and offered thoughts, challenges, and critiques. This study of Galatians was made all the stronger for your contributions.

Expanding the video series into this book has been a long process of discovery and learning, and I've enjoyed every minute of it. It is a journey I could not have made on my own. I want to acknowledge and thank Dale Williams, Serena DeKryger, Daniel Saxton, and the team at Zondervan for their enduring professionalism and positivity. Dale, in particular, was a champion, giving form and direction to this book and providing encouragement to its second-guessing, naively enthusiastic author.

Benjamin Franklin reportedly quipped, "Originality is the art of concealing your sources." Indeed, this book is nothing but a record of what I've learned from others. (Which is, itself, a line I borrowed from Timothy Keller!) I want to acknowledge the contributions of the many erudite pastors, scholars, and authors I have quoted on these pages who have helped to shape my Christian faith. These include Bruce Gore, Moisés Silva, R. Alan Cole, C. S. Lewis,

Sinclair Ferguson, Andrew Knowles, David Rudolph, Ralph Martin, Dietrich Bonhoeffer, Donald Hagner, Keith Stanglin, Wilfred Knox, G. K. Chesterton, Michael Heiser, and Augustine. I have had the honor of meeting and speaking with some of these thinkers. All have informed, challenged, and expanded my thinking.

God has also blessed me with a number of wise, generous, and godly mentors and friends who have encouraged and supported me. They have offered valuable feedback and guidance on my apologetics ministry in general and this book in particular. I am deeply thankful to Alan Newlove, Tony Calabrese, Dick Wells, Paul Guffey, Ron Brown, Tim and Shelly Sassen, Eric Mason, and Chad Bird.

> I thank my God every time I remember you. In all my prayers for all of you, I always pray with joy because of your partnership in the gospel from the first day until now, being confident of this, that he who began a good work in you will carry it on to completion until the day of Christ Jesus. (Phil. 1:3–6)

Lastly, I want to thank my brilliant and beautiful wife, Debra, who believes in me even when it doesn't make sense and is brave enough to hold my rebellious feet to the fire when I need it.

NOTES

Why Galatians Matters Today

1. After wrestling all night with Jacob, God declared, "Your name will no longer be Jacob, but Israel, because you have struggled with God and with humans and have overcome" (Gen. 32:28). And Jacob, of course, was the father of the twelve tribes of Israel. For an extended example of wrestling with God, read the books of Job or Ecclesiastes.
2. Deuteronomy 6:5; Matthew 22:37; Mark 12:30; Luke 10:27.

Introduction

1. All Scripture citations are from Galatians unless otherwise indicated.
2. I use the term "mainstream Christianity" to refer to the general theological convictions shared by all flavors of Protestantism.
3. Acts 11:2; Galatians 2:12; Titus 1:10.
4. Pronounced: *you-dye-EE-zoh*.
5. Genesis 3:15; Deuteronomy 18:15; Luke 24:44; John 5:39–40; 8:56.

The Shape and Setting of Galatians

1. Our modern chapter divisions were developed around 1227 by the archbishop of Canterbury, Stephen Langton. The first Bible to use this chapter numbering was the Wycliffe English Bible of 1382. Since that time, nearly all Bible translations have followed Langton's chapter divisions.
2. This phrase is also found in 1 Corinthians 9:21.

3. This is the only place in the Bible where this phrase is used.

4. Paul (*Paulus*) was his Roman name. His Hebrew name was Saul (*Sha'ul*).

5. Most likely the church in Antioch.

6. The ancient Gallic tribes (Gauls) lived primarily in the region of modern France. However, their conquests brought them as far as Anatolia, also known as Asia Minor (modern-day Turkey).

7. See 1 Corinthians 3:16–17 and 1 Peter 2:5, 9.

8. Acts 9:1–19.

9. The term *TaNaKh* is an acronym derived from the first letters of the three main sections of the Hebrew Bible: *Torah* (Law), *Nevi'im* (Prophets), and *Ketuvim* (Writings).

10. The Hebrew word *mashiach* (messiah) and the Greek word *Christos* (Christ) both mean "anointed one." Both are used to refer to the same Person. So, whenever we encounter the word *Christ*—which appears more than 500 times in the NT—we can mentally replace it with the word *Messiah*. Doing so can help us view Jesus in His true, historical Hebrew role.

11. Moisés Silva, "Galatians," in *New Bible Commentary: 21st Century Edition*, ed. D. A. Carson, R. T. France, J. A. Motyer, and G. J. Wenham, 4th ed. (Leicester, UK; Downers Grove: InterVarsity Press, 1994), 1206.

12. Acts 9:2; 19:9; 19:23; 24:14, 22.

13. Mark J. Keown, *Discovering the New Testament: An Introduction to Its Background, Theology, and Themes*, vol. 1: *The Gospels & Acts* (Bellingham, WA: Lexham, 2018), 366.

14. A. Sabatier in Marvin Richardson Vincent, *Word Studies in the New Testament*, vol. 4 (New York: Charles Scribner's Sons, 1887), 79–80.

Called by God (Galatians 1:1–24)

1. Larry W. Hurtado, *Destroyer of the Gods: Early Christian Distinctiveness in the Roman World* (Waco, TX: Baylor University Press, 2016), 105–6.

2. Harry Y. Gamble, *Books and Readers in the Early Church: A History of Early Christian Texts* (New Haven: Yale University Press, 1997), 112.

3. Deuteronomy 5:22–27.

4. Exodus 25:8–9; 29:43–46.

5. Gary Dorrien, *The Making of American Liberal Theology: Imagining Progressive Religion, 1805–1900* (Louisville: Westminster John Knox Press, 2001), xiii.

6. Romans 11:13; Galatians 2:8; Ephesians 3:8.

Paul and the Apostles (Galatians 2:1–14)

1. In Jewish categories, one is always said to go "up" to Jerusalem. Pastor Aaron Koch notes, "Traveling to Jerusalem involved a journey up in altitude. But Jerusalem was also theologically 'up.' For that's where the temple of God was, where His name was present for their blessing. So whether you were coming from the north or the south on a map, you were going up, to the place where God was for you." See Aaron Koch, "Going Up to Jerusalem," Mt. Zion Lutheran Church, March 25, 2023, https://www.mount ziongreenfield.org/posts/sermon/going-up-to-jerusalem/.

2. Geerhardus Vos, "Hebrews, the Epistle of the Diatheke" in *The Princeton Theological Review* (Jan. 1916), 59.

3. See also John 13:35; 15:12, 17.

4. Although the earliest manuscripts do not include the text of John 7:53–8:11, I believe in the authenticity of this story insofar as it contains spiritual truths and accords with the body of Christ's teachings.

5. Sinclair Ferguson, *The Whole Christ: Legalism, Antinomianism, and Gospel Assurance—Why the Marrow Controversy Still Matters* (Wheaton: Crossway, 2016), 156.

Paul Opposes Peter (Galatians 2:11–14)

1. Matthew 9:10–17; Mark 2:15–22; Luke 5:29–39.

2. R. L. Solberg, *What God Has Made Clean: Why Christians Are Not Required to Eat Kosher* (Nashville: Boyle & Co., 2023), 20–21.

3. This event is also recorded in Mark 7:1–23.

4. Land animals with divided hoofs that chew their cud are clean, as are water creatures with fins and scales. When it comes to birds and insects, we're only given a list.

5. Matthew 15:1–20; Mark 7:1–23.

6. There's something about Peter, Jesus, and threes. Peter denied Jesus three times, as Jesus had prophesied (Matt. 26:34, 74–75; Luke 22:34, 60; John 13:38; 18:27). Jesus told Peter three times, "What God has made clean, do not call common" (Acts 10:9–26 ESV). Jesus asked Peter three times, "Do you love me?" (John 21:15–17).

7. Peter and his brother Andrew were the first men Jesus called to follow Him.

8. Andrew Knowles, *The Bible Guide: An All-in-One Introduction to the Book of Books* (Minneapolis: Augsburg, 2001), 606.

Justified by Faith (Galatians 2:15–21)

1. Paul makes this very point in Romans 4:4–5.

2. These old covenant atonement rituals are spelled out in Leviticus 16.

3. Romans 6:10; Hebrews 7:27; 9:12, 26; 10:10.

4. Christians who consider themselves "Torah-observant" participate in old covenant rituals such as observing the seven Torah feasts, the seventh day Sabbath, and eating kosher. They believe that these things are required of followers of Jesus and not keeping them is sinful. This belief system is broadly referred to as "Torahism." While the Torah is a beautiful and fundamental part of the Christian faith, Torah-*ism* is a dangerous misapplication of the old covenant law.

5. R. Alan Cole, *The Epistle of Paul to the Galatians: An Introduction and Commentary*, Tyndale New Testament Commentaries 9 (Downers Grove: InterVarsity Press, 1989), 123.

Faith or Works of the Law? (Galatians 3:1–14)

1. The Abrahamic covenant did not just mention that Abraham would have descendants who would become a nation and a blessing to the world. It also included God's promise to give Abraham and his descendants the land of Canaan (Gen. 12:1, 7; 13:14–17; 15:5; 17:2–5). In Galatians, however, Paul does not speak of the promised land.

2. "The Augustinian formulation *Novum Testamentum in Vetere latet, Vetus in Novo patet,* [translates to] "The New is in the Old concealed, the Old is in the New revealed." See Al Wolters, "The History of Old Testament Interpretation: An Anecdotal Survey," in *Hearing the Old Testament: Listening for God's Address,* ed. Craig G. Bartholomew and David J. H. Beldman (Grand Rapids: Eerdmans, 2012), 26.

3. Chad Bird, *The Christ Key: Unlocking the Centrality of Christ in the Old Testament* (Irvine, CA: New Reformation, 2021), vii. Emphasis in the original.

4. For example, when asked which commandment in the law was the greatest, Jesus responded by citing Deuteronomy 6:5 and Leviticus 19:18, concluding, "All the Law and the Prophets hang on these two commandments" (Matt. 22:40).

5. David Rudolph, "One New Man, Hebrew Roots, Replacement Theology," The King's Collective, July 29, 2024, https://collective.tku.edu/wp-content/uploads/2024/07/1-DR-One-New-Man_-Hebrew-Roots_-Replacement-Theology-revised-7_29_24.pdf.

6. See also Romans 2:23; 3:27; 4:2; Ephesians 2:9.

7. Matthew 9:22, 29; Mark 5:34; 10:52; Luke 7:50; 8:48; 17:19; 18:42.

8. Matthew 9:22.

9. Matthew 9:2; Mark 2:5; Luke 5:20.

10. Matthew 8:10; 15:28.

11. Matthew 17:20; Luke 17:6.

12. The Hebrew word *midrash* means "study, interpretation, exposition."

13. Tony Calabrese, "Easter Sunday 2023," COTC Spring Hill,

sermon on April 10, 2023, YouTube video, 1:44:52, https://www
.youtube.com/watch?v=344Oanpy_cg/.

14. Ralph P. Martin, "Galatians," in *The New Testament Page by Page*,
ed. Martin Manser, Open Your Bible Commentary (Creative 4
International, 2018), 692.

15. These figures of speech (called *metonyms*) are common in Paul's
writings. For example, he often uses "the cross" to refer to the
entire work of Christ's atonement, "flesh" to refer to fallen human
nature, and "circumcised" and "uncircumcised" to refer to Jews
and Gentiles, respectively.

The Law and the Promise (Galatians 3:15–29)

1. Circumcision was given to Abraham and his descendants as a sign
of this covenant, and those males who refused it were to be cut off
from the family. But doing so did not break the covenant itself.
Rather, it resulted in the offender being ejected from the covenant.

2. Exodus 19:5–6; 24:7–8; Deuteronomy 7:11–12.

3. "One Law, Two Sticks: A Critical Look at the Hebrew Roots
Movement," IAMCS, January 15, 2014, 4–5, https://www.iamcs
.org/wp-content/uploads/2023/06/One_Law_Two_Sticks.pdf.

4. G. Walter Hansen, *Galatians*, The IVP New Testament
Commentary Series (Downers Grove: InterVarsity Press, 1994), 102.

5. The Talmud teaches that every Jewish man must recite three
blessings daily (Tosefta Berakhot 6:18). They express gratitude
in the negative: Thank God that I am not a gentile, a woman, or
a slave. These statements, often called the "blessings of identity,"
eventually became part of the daily morning service.

6. Timothy Keller, *The Reason for God: Belief in an Age of Skepticism*
(New York: Riverhead Books, 2008), 187.

Children and Heirs (Galatians 4:1–20)

1. The phrase in Greek is *stoicheia tou kosmou*.

2. Paul uses the term "sonship" to connect the idea to God's Son. But,

of course, the concept applies to both men and women: "There is neither Jew nor Gentile, neither slave nor free, nor is there male and female, for you are all one in Christ Jesus" (3:28).

3. Matthew 26:28; Mark 14:24; Luke 22:20; 1 Corinthians 11:25; Hebrews 13:20.

4. Revelation 1:6; 5:10; 20:6.

5. In the Bible, a "proselyte" refers to a non-Israelite who has converted to Judaism. The term itself originates from the Greek word *prosēlytos*, which means "a stranger" or "one who has come over." This term describes Gentiles (non-Jews) who have embraced the Jewish faith and its practices.

6. See 1 Corinthians 4:16; 11:1; Philippians 3:17.

7. Hans Dieter Betz, *Galatians: A Commentary on Paul's Letter to the Churches in Galatia*, Hermeneia (Philadelphia: Fortress Press, 1979), 220.

8. Dietrich Bonhoeffer, *The Cost of Discipleship* (New York: Touchstone, 1995), 44–45.

9. This is point #5 from their "Brief Biblical Case for LGBTQ Inclusion": https://reformationproject.org/biblical-case.

10. Matthew Vines, *God and the Gay Christian: The Biblical Case in Support of Same-Sex Relationships* (New York: Convergent, 2015), 129–30.

11. Ellen G. White, *Evangelism* (Washington, D.C.: Review and Herald, 1946), 235.2, https://m.egwwritings.org/en/book/30.1246?hl.

12. Warren W. Wiersbe, *The Bible Exposition Commentary*, vol. 1 (Wheaton: Victor, 1996), 708. Emphasis in original.

The Allegory of Sarah and Hagar (Galatians 4:21–31)

1. Gamaliel was a first-century rabbi still hailed as one of the greatest teachers in the history of Judaism. He was a leading authority in the Sanhedrin and the grandson of the great Jewish teacher Hillel the Elder.

2. Luke 24:44–48; Galatians 1:11–12.

3. Keith D. Stanglin, *The Letter and the Spirit of Biblical Interpretation: From the Early Church to Modern Practice* (Grand Rapids: Baker Academic, 2018), 21.

4. Donald A. Hagner, *Encountering the Book of Hebrews* (Grand Rapids: Baker Academic, 2002), 31–32.

5. The story of Abraham, Sarah, and Hagar is found in Genesis 16–18 and 21.

6. Interestingly, this is the same Hebrew root word from which we get the name "Isaac." Ishmael was "Isaac-ing" his new brother.

7. See page 62.

8. If you're reading a Bible with cross-references, it will show you which OT passage is being quoted in the NT. It can be quite enriching (and even eye-opening) to read the entire OT chapter from which the cited passage was taken.

9. R. Alan Cole, *The Epistle of Paul to the Galatians: An Introduction and Commentary*, Tyndale New Testament Commentaries 9 (Downers Grove: InterVarsity Press, 1989), 183.

10. Warren W. Wiersbe, *The Bible Exposition Commentary*, vol. 1 (Wheaton: Victor, 1996), 709–711.

Freedom in Christ (Galatians 5:1–12)

1. See Genesis 27:40; Exodus 6:6–7; Leviticus 26:13; Numbers 25:3–5; Deuteronomy 28:48, etc.

2. Mackie outlines these patterns in "Abraham, the Immigrant, and Circumcision," *BibleProject* (podcast), December 14, 2020, https://bibleproject.com/podcast/abraham-immigrant-and-circumcision/.

3. Some argue that circumcision is still required for Jewish followers of Jesus but not for Gentiles. However, that would introduce two different standards of obedience for Christians, which the Bible does not support. Case in point, Paul's argument in Galatians 5:2–6 leaves no room for a "two law" approach on this issue.

4. Walter Bauer, F. W. Danker, W. F. Arndt, and F. W. Gingrich, eds., *A Greek-English Lexicon of the New Testament and Other Early*

Christian Literature, 3rd ed. (Chicago: University of Chicago Press, 2000), 525.

Life by the Spirit (Galatians 5:13–25)

1. Nicole Spector, "When Lottery Riches Lead to Ruin: Eight Winners Whose Luck Ran Out," NBC News, January 13, 2016, https://www.nbcnews.com/better/money/when-lottery-riches-lead-ruin-eight-winners-whose-luck-ran-n495826/.

2. Steve Mcvicker, "Unlucky Strike," *Dallas Observer*, February 10, 2000, https://www.dallasobserver.com/news/unlucky-strike-6406997/.

3. We looked at the Torah's requirements for annual sin atonement in the section called "A Closer Look at Justification" on pages 45–51.

4. See John 3:16–17; Romans 3:28; 4:5; 5:1; Galatians 2:16; 3:11, 24; 5:4; Ephesians 1:13; Philippians 3:9, etc.

5. The NIV translation mitigates this issue by translating the Greek word *dikaioō* as "considered righteous" rather than "justified." The apparent contradiction between Paul and James is more pronounced in other translations.

6. See *Merriam-Webster*, s.v., "justify," accessed August 20, 2024, https://www.merriam-webster.com/dictionary/justify/.

7. The word *dikaioō* can additionally mean (1) to take up a legal cause, (2) to vindicate, and (3) to cause someone to be released from personal or institutional claims (to make free/pure). See Walter Bauer, F. W. Danker, W. F. Arndt, and F. W. Gingrich, eds., *A Greek-English Lexicon of the New Testament and Other Early Christian Literature*, 3rd ed. (Chicago: University of Chicago Press, 2000), 249.

8. Bruce Gore, "Freedom or Self-Indulgence?," sermon, accessed May 20, 2023, http://76.147.183.224/Audio/PaulsLetters04.mp3.

9. Andrew Knowles, *The Bible Guide: An All-in-One Introduction to the Book of Books* (Minneapolis: Augsburg, 2001), 611.

10. Romans 6:10; Hebrews 7:27; 9:12, 26; 10:1–18.

11. Wilfred L. Knox, "Galatians," in *A New Commentary on Holy Scripture: Including the Apocrypha*, ed. Charles Gore, Henry Leighton Goudge, and Alfred Guillaume, vol. 3 (New York: Macmillan, 1942), 537.

12. G. K. Chesterton, *Orthodoxy* (New York: John Lane, 1908), 175–76.

Bearing One Another's Burdens (Galatians 6:1–10)

1. Christopher Cone, *Applied Biblical Worldview: Essays on Christian Ethics* (Fort Worth, TX: Exegetica, 2016), 39. Emphasis original.

2. Bonhoeffer discusses this concept in his influential book *The Cost of Discipleship* (1937). He was a German pastor and theologian and an outspoken critic of Hitler's dictatorship, Nazi ideology, and the church's complacency during the rise of fascism. Just weeks before the end of World War II, Bonhoeffer was executed by the Nazis because of his involvement in a conspiracy to assassinate Adolf Hitler and overthrow the Nazi regime.

3. See Acts 9:16; 2 Corinthians 11:28–33; Galatians 6:17; Philippians 1:29–30; 2 Timothy 1:11–12; 2:8–9; 3:10–11.

4. See Romans 12:18–21 for the fuller context.

A Final Warning & Benediction (Galatians 6:11–18)

1. See 1 Corinthians 16:21; Colossians 4:18; 2 Thessalonians 3:17; Philemon 19.

2. Uncial is handwriting in a large script where all the letters are the same height. It was especially used in Greek and Latin manuscripts.

3. Robert Jamieson, A. R. Fausset, and David Brown, *Commentary Critical and Explanatory on the Whole Bible*, vol. 2 (Oak Harbor, WA: Logos Research Systems, 1997), 339.

4. Most other English translations translate *kai* as "and" in this verse, including the CEB, ESV, KJV, LSB, LEB, NASB, NET, and NRSV.

5. Galatians 2:4; 4:3, 7–8, 24–25, 31; 5:1.

Conclusion

1. C. S. Lewis, *Mere Christianity* (New York: HarperOne, 2001), 28.
2. See all of Matthew 23 to understand how strongly Jesus dealt with the Pharisees and the teachers of the law.